Good Morning, Kimchi!

Good Morning, Kimchi!

by Sook-ja Yoon

Translated by Young-hie Han

HOLLYM

Elizabeth, NJ · Seoul

First published in 2005
Second printing, 2006
by Hollym International Corp.
18 Donald Place, Elizabeth, New Jersey 07208, USA
Phone: (908)353-1655 Fax: (908)353-0255
http://www.hollym.com

Published simultaneously in Korea
by Hollym Corp., Publishers
13-13 Gwancheol-dong, Jongno-gu, Seoul 110-111, Korea
Phone: (82 2)735-7551~4 Fax: (82 2)730-5149, 8192
http://www.hollym.co.kr e-mail: info@hollym.co.kr

ISBN : 1-56591-216-0
Library of Congress Control Number : 2005923990

Printed in Korea

Abbreviations

ea : each	g : gram
kg : kilogram	l : liter
ts : tea spoon	Ts : table spoon
tss : tea spoons	Tss : table spoons

PREFACE

I am extremely happy that this book has now been translated into English, as well as another version that has been translated into Japanese, as people around the world are eating kimchi more than ever before.

This book is an abridged version of my Korean book *Good Morning, Kimchi!: 111 Kinds of Kimchi.* Along with traditional kimchi recipes, there are many modern kimchi recipes throughout this book which use vegetables that people in other countries will be more familiar with. It is my sincere hope that people who read this book will have kimchi become one of their favorite dishes in the future as a result of the recipes contained within.

Due to its strong, spicy smell and hot taste, people from other countries have traditionally been hesitant to try kimchi. However, those who have tried it will be the first to admit that appearances can be deceiving, because kimchi is actually very delicious. More than that, kimchi has long been known to be a very healthy food, but recently it has come to light that it may also help prevent certain types of Severe Acute Respiratory Syndrome (SARS). The fact that no Koreans have, to date, been infected with the SARS virus is, some believe, directly attributable to the fact that kimchi is a staple with every Korean meal. According to Prof. Sa-wook Kang of Seoul National University, a lactic acid called leuconostoc, something that is very prevalent in kimchi, has been found to neutralize the SARS virus. In his experiments, most chickens that were infected with the SARS virus actually survived after being treated with leuconostoc-rich kimchi.

Koreans have a variety of kimchi that they eat, depending on the time of year, the occasion, the region, the meal, and the person's tastes. Today, there are approximately 200 different kinds of kimchi, many of which are covered in this book. In a world where people are getting fed up with fast, greasy and otherwise unhealthy food that leads to obesity and other serious medical conditions, kimchi is the perfect alternative. Kimchi is rich in fiber, minerals, amino acids (some of which are only produced during the fermentation process), and vitamins, especially vitamin C. Kimchi goes well with rice and many other dietary foods. Yet it also goes well with oily food, as it mitigates the harmful effects greasy food can have on the mouth, throat and stomach. By removing most traces of unpleasant grease in the digestive tract, kimchi helps the digestion process, for it contains a great many beneficial microbes.

Personally, kimchi has and always will be an integral part of my diet. When I was young, especially during the Korean War (1950-53) and in the ensuing years afterward, people were forced to live hand-to-mouth. At such times, rice, along with kimchi, which was an important source of vitamin C when fresh vegetables were not easy to come by, was a favorite dish of many Koreans. However, in the years since then when Korea began its ascension to its present position of economic wealth and prosperity, people stopped eating kimchi as much, turning instead to greasy, unhealthy food. Nowadays, though, people —especially the young— are rediscovering how great kimchi is once again.

I am much obliged to many people for the work they did on *Good Morning, Kimchi!.* While putting this book together, I had to call on many friends and colleagues for assistance. I would like to thank all of them now. First of all, Myung-sook Lee, assistant director of the Institute of Traditional Food, provided me with a great deal of data for this book, not to mention the information from experiments she carried out with foreign vegetables, which proved invaluable to some of the kimchi recipes in this book. Kwang-seok Noh, head researcher at the Institute, was kind enough to look through the text carefully, making it a better book as a result. I would also like to thank Young-hie Han, who translated this book from Korean to English, and who had to make many drafts along the way because of changes I made to the original draft. Finally, I wish to thank Ki-man Ham of Hollym Publishers for taking the time to publish this book, even though he has published similar books on the same topic. My thanks also to Hui-jeong Yi, who handled the actual editing of this book, and to Na-eun Kwon, who carried out the proofreading of this book in Korean with the utmost care, paying careful attention to the coherence of all the relevant terms along the way.

CONTENTS

Part III

Fusion Kimchi

Part I
Introduction

I. A History of Kimchi

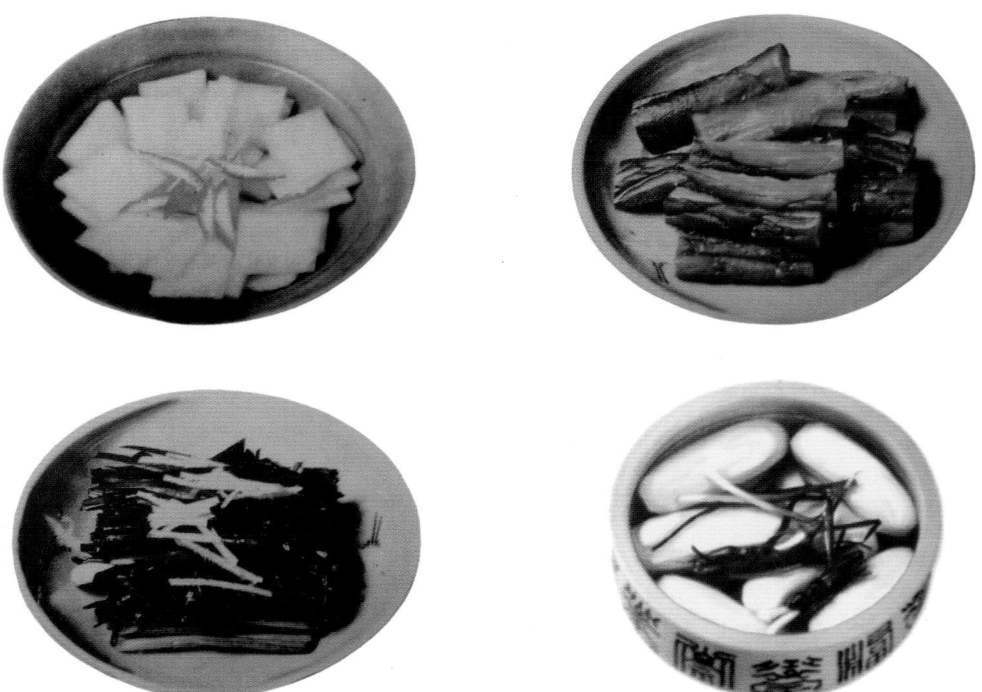

Kimchi is the best known fermented Korean food. From earlier times, Koreans have made kimchi with various vegetables and seasonings in many different ways, preserved and stored it for a long period of time in the cold season, and enjoyed it with rice and other grains. The first written record of kimchi appeared in the middle of the Goryeo dynasty (935-1392). In *Donggugisanggukjip*, a collection of writings by Lee Gyu-bo, a poem called "*Gapoyugyeong*" (Six Songs on the Backyard Vegetable Plot) records the following: "Preserved in soybean paste kimchi tastes good in the summer, whereas kimchi pickled in brine is served as a good side dish during the winter. When the root of the Chinese cabbage grows larger in the ground, it tastes like a pear, especially after the first frost in the autumn harvest season." This is the first mention of kimchi being pickled in brine.

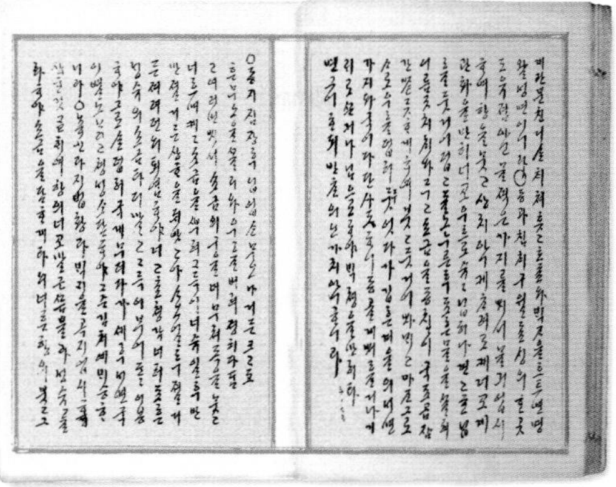

In 1670, a woman known only as Mrs. Chang of Andong illustrated seven kinds of kimchi in her book *Eumsik Jimibang* (Ways of Knowing the Tastes of Food), in which the pheasant was included among kimchi is many different ingredients. This is evidence that protein was included in kimchi's from at least the 17th century on. One of modern-day kimchi's most important ingredients, red pepper, came into use after the Hideyoshi invasions (1592-1598), when Japan invaded Korea during the Joseon dynasty. A more concrete record is found in *Jeungbo Sallimgyeongje* (Revised Forestry Economy), which affirmed that red pepper came to hold a firm root in kimchi making.

From that time on, the appearance and the fermentation of kimchi have changed drastically because of the introduction of red pepper. Furthermore, Koreans' inclination of favoring the color red, along with the cultivation of the of the spicy red pepper, contributed to the basic form and character of present day kimchi. Later, a woman known only as Ms. Lee of Binheogag mentioned for the first time in the *Gyuhapchongseo* (A Reference Book for Women) the use of fermented fish in kimchi. Then, in 1827, ninety-two kinds of kimchi were illustrated in minute detail in Seo Yu-Gu's *Imwongyeongjesibyukji* (Sixteen Records of Forest and Fields). From this book, we can conclude that most of the present day forms of Korean kimchi had already been established by this time.

Today, there are more then 200 different varities of kimchi, many of which have become an indispensable part of every Korean meal.

2. Kimchi, A Scientifically Proven Wholesome Food

Through the interaction of the main ingredients of kimchi, Chinese cabbage and radish, along with the various species and seasonings, a particular kimchi taste is produced as the fermentation process is carried out.

Kimchi is low in sugar and fat. Therefore it is low in calories, but rich in vitamins, minerals and fiber. It used to provide an essential source of vitamin C during the winter when fresh vegetables were scarce. The garlic used in kimchi is regarded as an invigorating element and good for recuperation from fatigue. Its allicin contents combine with vitamin B1 to help the latter become easily absorbed into the body. The fermented fish juice and other marine products contain a great deal of protein which dissolves into amino acids during fermentation. As well, calcium from the bones of fish that is absorbed into the seasonings of kimchi becomes a good source of the calcium our body needs.

Kimchi has also proven to be very effective in preventing colon cancer, obesity and high blood pressure, while helping keep the bowels clean. It stimulates the secretion of pepsin in the stomach, and stirs the digestion and absorption of food in the bowels as it maintains the balance of microbes there.

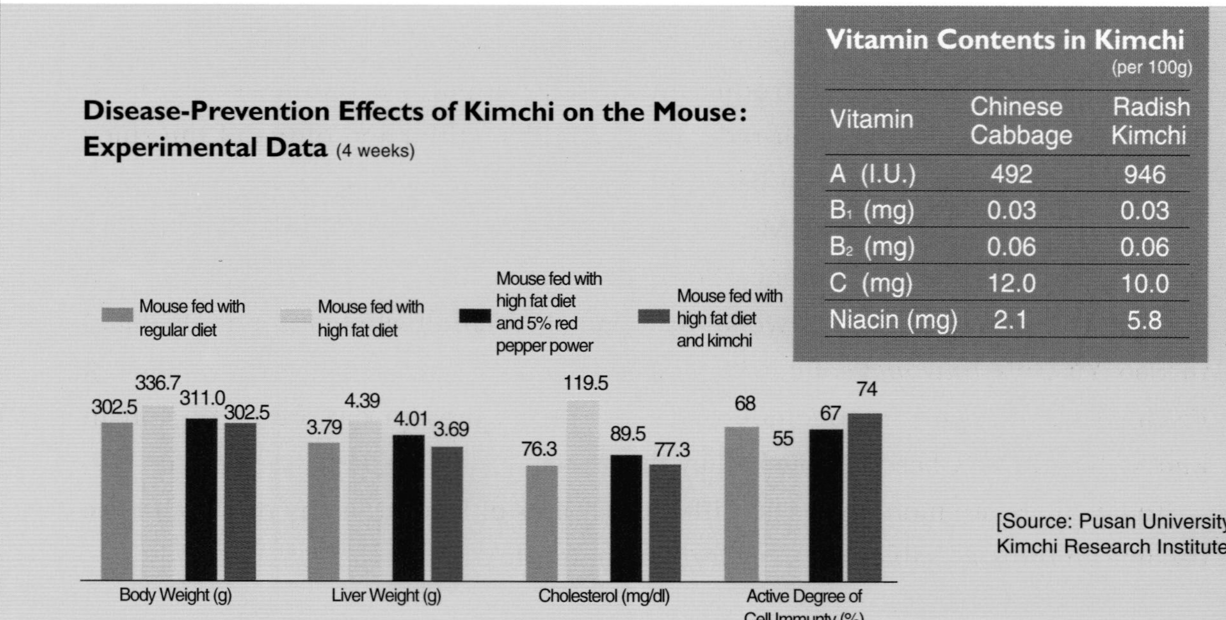

Vitamin Contents in Kimchi (per 100g)

Vitamin	Chinese Cabbage	Radish Kimchi
A (I.U.)	492	946
B_1 (mg)	0.03	0.03
B_2 (mg)	0.06	0.06
C (mg)	12.0	10.0
Niacin (mg)	2.1	5.8

[Source: Pusan University Kimchi Research Institute]

* Codex Standard for Kimchi

1 SCOPE

This Standard applies the product known as kimchi, as defined in Section 2 below, which is prepared with Chinese cabbage as a predominant ingredient and other vegetables which have been trimmed, cut, salted and seasoned before fermentation.

2 DESCRIPTION

2.1 PRODUCT DEFINITION

Kimchi is the product:

a) prepared from varieties of Chinese cabbage, Brassica pekinensis Rupr.; such Chinese cabbages shall be free from significant defects, and trimmed to remove inedible parts, salted, washed with fresh water, and drained to remove excess water; they may or may not be cut into suitable sized pieces/parts;

b) processed with seasoning mixture mainly consisting of red pepper (Capsicum annuum L.) powder, garlic, ginger, edible Allium varieties other than garlic, and radish. These ingredients may be chopped, sliced and broken into pieces; and

c) fermented before or after being packaged into appropriate containers to ensure the proper ripening and preservation of the product by lactic acid production at low temperatures.

2.2 STYLES

The product should be presented in one of the following styles:

a) Whole:	whole Chinese cabbage;
b) Halves:	Chinese cabbages divided lengthwise into halves;
c) Quarters:	Chinese cabbages divided lengthwise into quarters; and
d) Slices or Chips:	Chinese cabbage leaves cut into pieces of 1~6 cm in length and width

3 ESSENTIAL COMPOSITION AND QUALITY FACTORS

3.1 COMPOSITION

3.1.1 Basic Ingredients

a) Chinese cabbages and the seasoning mixture as described in Section 2;

b) salt (sodium chloride).

3.1.2 Other Permitted Ingredients

a) fruits;

b) vegetables other than those described in Section 2;

c) sesame seeds;

d) nuts;

e) sugars (carbohydrate sweeteners);

f) salted and fermented seafood;

g) glutinous rice paste;

h) wheat flour paste.

3.1.3 Other Composition

a) Total acidity (as lactic acid)	not more than 1.0% m/m
b) Salt (sodium chloride) content	1.0~4.0% m/m
c) Mineral impurities	not more than 0.03% m/m

3.2 QUALITY CRITERIA

Kimchi shall have normal flavour, odour and colour and shall possess texture characteristic of the product.

3.2.1 Other Quality Criteria

a) Colour: The product should have red colour originating from red pepper.

b) Taste: The product should have hot and salty taste. It may also have sour taste.

c) Texture: The product should be reasonably firm, crisp, and chewy.

4 FOOD ADDITIVES

Only those food additives listed below may be used within the limits specified.

No	Name of Food Additive	Maximum Level
4.1 ACIDITY REGULATORS		
269	Acetic acid	Limited by GMP
270	Lactic acid	
330	Citric acid	
4.2 FLAVOURINGS		
	Natural flavours and nature-identical flavours, as defined in the *Codex Alimentarius,* Volume 1A	Limited by GMP
4.3 FLAVOUR ENHANCERS		
621	Monosodium L-glutamate	Limited by GMP
627	Disodium 5'-guanylate	
631	Disodium 5'-inosinate	
4.4 TEXTURIZERS		
420	Sorbitol	Limited by GMP
4.5 THICKENING AND STABILIZING AGENTS		
407	Carrageenan (including furcellaran)	Limited by GMP
415	Xanthan gum	

5 CONTAMINANTS

5.1 HEAVY METALS

The products covered by the provisions of this Standard shall comply with those maximum levels for heavy metals established by the Codex Alimentarius Commission for these products.

5.2 PESTICIDE RESIDUES

The products covered by the provisions of this Standard shall comply with those maximum residue limits established by the Codex Alimentarius Commission for these products.

6 HYGIENE

6.1 It is recommended that the products covered by the provisions of this Standard be prepared and handled in accordance with the appropriate sections of the Recommended International Code of Practice – General Principles of Food Hygiene (CAC/RCP 1-1969, Rev. 3-1997), and other relevant Codex texts such as Codes of Hygienic Practice and Codes of Practice.

6.2 The products should comply with any microbiological criteria established in accordance with the Principles for the Establishment and Application of Microbiological Criteria for Foods (CAC/GL 21-1997).

7 WEIGHT AND MEASURES

7.1 FILL OF CONTAINER

7.1.1 Minimum Drained Weight

The drained weight of the final product, as a percent of the indicated weight, shall not be less than 80% by weight.

8 LABELLING

8.1 Kimchi shall be labelled in accordance with the Codex General Standard for the Labelling of Prepackaged Foods (CODEX STAN 1-1985, Rev. 1-1991).

8.2 THE NAME OF THE PRODUCT

The name of the product shall be "Kimchi". The style should be included in close proximity to the name of the product.

8.3 LABELLING OF NON-RETAIL CONTAINERS

Information required in Sections 4.1-4.8 of the Codex General Standard for the Labelling of Prepackaged Foods and storage instructions if necessary shall be given either on the container or in accompanying documents, except that the name of the product, lot identification, and the name and address of the manufacturer, packer, distributor and/or importer, shall appear on the container. However, lot identification, and the name and address of the manufacturer, packer, distributor and/or importer may be replaced by an identification mark, provided that such a mark is clearly identifiable with the accompanying documents.

9 METHODS OF ANALYSIS AND SAMPLING See Codex Alimentarius Volume 13.

[Source: Codex Alimentarius Commission]

3. Pickling/Salting Chinese Cabbage and Processing

Pickling Cabbage

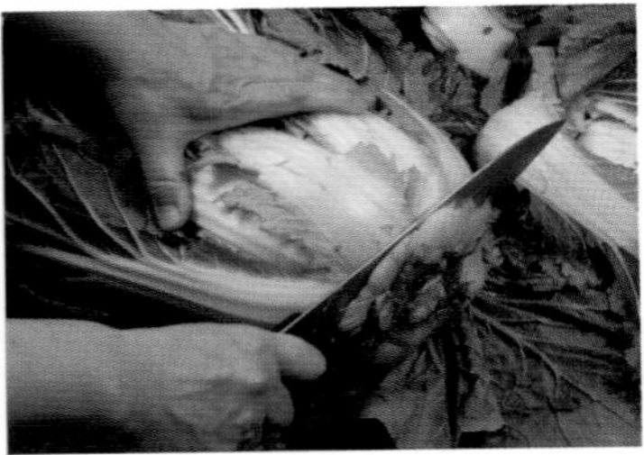

1. Remove the coarse yellow outer leaves of the Chinese cabbage and cut off as much of its root as possible.

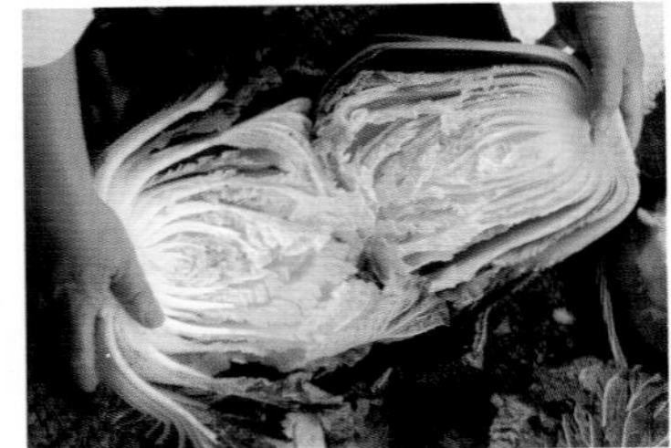

2. Cut the cabbage lengthwise down the middle with a knife, from the root to the halfway point (approx. 10 cm), then split the remaining portion into two separate halves.

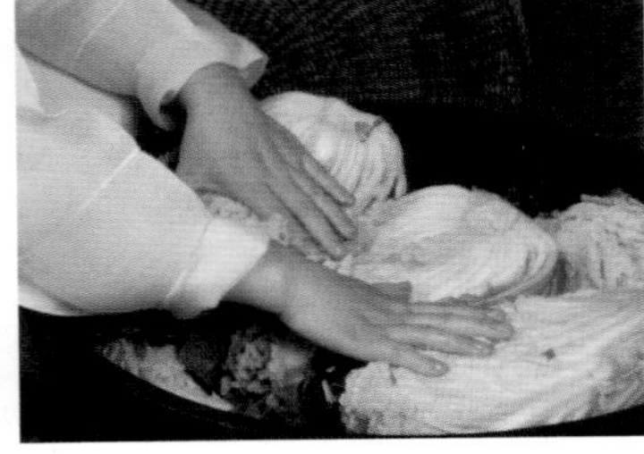

3. Prepare water that is 15 percent salt water and then preserve the Chinese cabbage for 6-8 hours in this solution.

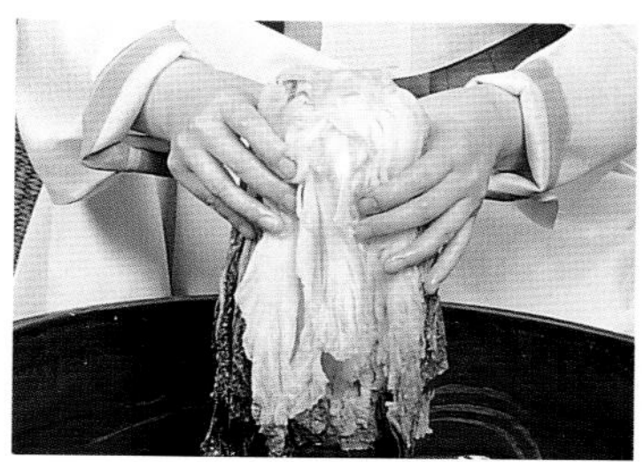

4. Wash the salted cabbage three or four times under running water, then drain the water by putting the cabbage on a flat basket for 30 minutes.

Preparation of Kimchi Ingredients

1. Trim the radish by slicing it into thin round pieces, which are cut into narrow strips (i.e. thin julienne).
2. The Welsh onion, glue plant, watercress, threaded green onion and other spices should be trimmed, washed and cut into 4-5 cm long pieces. Garlic and ginger should be ground finely for most kimchi, or thin-sliced for watery kimchi.
3. Pickled baby shrimp should be scooped from their juice and chopped minutely. Wash the fresh oysters and shrimp in mildly salty brine and then drain them. The fresh shrimp should be chopped roughly.
4. Add the same amount of water as salted anchovies to the salted anchovies themselves. The diluted salted anchovies are then boiled for ten minutes and filtered through a fine sieve to get a clean anchovy juice.

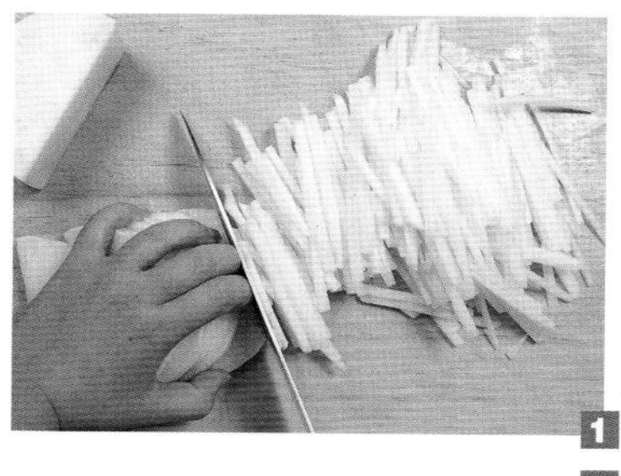

1 2
3 4

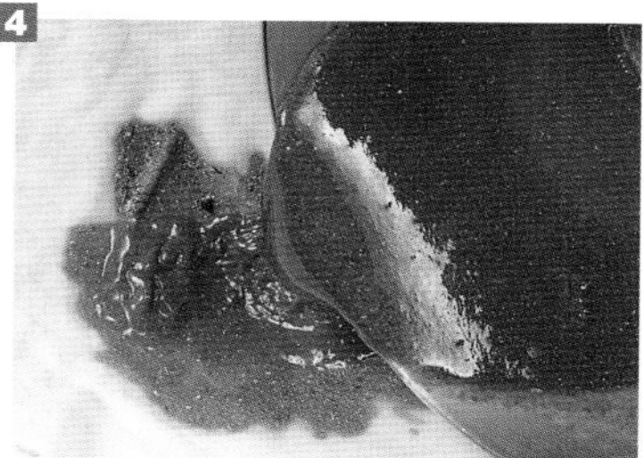

How to Make Cabbage Kimchi

1. Soak the red pepper powder thoroughly in the salted anchovy juice. The radish julienne then becomes coated sufficiently with this soaked red pepper powder.

2. Place the remaining spices with the radish julienne. Mix them together, slowly at first and then faster. Add the fresh shrimp and oysters, and mix thoroughly.

3. Put the spice mix between the leaves of the cabbage, coating each leaf entirely. The middle of the cabbage should be bound by its outer leaves in case any of the seasonings fall out.

4. Stack the stuffed cabbages in a container so that 70~80% of the container is full. Kimchi juice is made with the residual seasoning mix and salt, then poured into the container. Cover the entire stack with the coarse salted outer leaves of the cabbage. Then press hard on the covered stack to remove any remaining air in it, and also to prevent it from taking in any air, which is one common way kimchi can be spoiled. Finally, scatter table salt over the cabbage leaves before covering the container.

4. Storing Kimchi

1. Kimchi should be stored at a low temperature. Around 5℃ is the optimal temperature to maintain the best taste of kimchi. Right after the kimchi is finished fermenting, it may be left at room temperature for one day, and then stored in the refrigerator for further fermentation. Alternatively, it may be stored in a specialized kimchi refrigerator to attain peak taste, something that has become very popular in Korea lately.
2. Press hard against the Chinese cabbage stack before storing it in an airtight container in order to remove any air between the bulks of the cabbage. Kimchi should not be handled with wet hands because this spoils the kimchi with the transfer of harmful bacteria from the skin to the cabbage.

Traditional kimchi storage, kimchi *gwang*

Present-day kimchi storage, the kimchi refrigerator

5. Kimchi Ingredients

Chinese Cabbage

The main ingredient of kimchi is Chinese cabbage, which is rich in vitamin C and calcium, and contains agents that stimulate salivation in the mouth, thus helping digestion and preventing constipation.

The bigger the spring and summer cabbages are, the better. However, a medium sized autumn cabbage, around 3 kg, is best. A shorter cabbage is better for making watery kimchi and fresh cabbage kimchi. When making this kind of kimchi, the green portion of the leaves should be larger, well preserved and also thin. The white stem of the leaf should be hard when pressed. The cross section of the root should be whitish. Besides the radish, the cabbage is the most important vegetable in Korea.

Avoid using a cabbage with any dark spots. For kimchi that you plan on wrapping, choose a cabbage with many green leaves; for white kimchi, choose a cabbage with thick, shorter leaves.

Radish

Along with the Chinese cabbage, the radish is the most important vegetable in Korea. It helps to suppress phlegm and prevent the common cold with its high dosage of vitamin C. It also contains a starch-digesting agent, diastase. A white radish with a fine outer skin and the fewest possible blemishes is considered ideal. When it is split apart, there should appear no holes on the round surface. When pounded as a whole on a chopping board by hand, the best radish is hard and gives off clear thudding sounds. A longer radish is not favored. The Korean radish is regarded as the optimal radish for making kimchi.

When choosing radishes, make sure you keep in mind which dish you will be preparing.

Radishes To Be Stored Long-term in *Gimjang*

Radishes that are half green all over are best, though dark green radishes are to be avoided. The best radishes for *gimjang* are somewhat spicy.

Radishes for Stuffing Chinese Cabbage

The ideal radish is large, and includes a hard body plus a good deal of moisture inside. This radish is usually shaped like a cylinder, with a green head and wide leaves. When cut into small, fine pieces, it can be added to seasoning or spices or simply put in between layers of kimchi to make it taste better. This is best eaten after the kimchi has fermented.

Radishes for Cube Radish Kimchi

Choose a hard, succulent and straight radish with fine skin, whose upper half is more white than green, this will allow you to make even-shaped cubes, and whose leaves are greener.

Radishes for *Dongchimi*

Choose a medium sized radish whose lower part is larger and whose leaves are greener. A small radish, though harder, is not as succulent.

Radishes for Ponytail Kimchi

Choose a small, hard and round ponytail radish, whose leaves are greener and whose outer skin of the root is thin, one whose entire root gradually slopes downward in shape. This kind of ponytail radish is very tasty.

Radishes for *Yeolmu* Kimchi

A soft young radish with shorter roots and fresh green leaves that are full of fuzz is best.

Welsh Onion, Wakegi Green Onion and Threaded Green Onion

Thickness separates green onions from Welsh onions, Wakegi green onions and threaded green onions. A fresh Welsh onion has a thick stalk for a root and not very long leaves. A good Wakegi green onion has a chubby head and traditionally has short leaves, making it a delicious vegetable and not too soft to eat. The Wakegi green onion is not longer than 30 cm in most instances. The color of the Wakegi green onion is often darker than the threaded green onion, and the shape of its root sticks to the stalk like a nail. The threaded green onion is pale green in color and is often thin. Its length is usually about 30 cm, with the root being flat and broad.

Watercress/Parsley

Watercress is a must in kimchi, especially in all watery kimchi, because of its characteristic scent and its ability to stimulate appetites. Known as an alkaline food item that is quite wholesome, good watercress is long and leafy, its stem fat and shiny. It should also be soft and fragrant. Watercress that shows a thin thread when its joint is torn apart should be avoided. Hot watercress is suitable for *gimjang* kimchi in autumn.

Glue Plant

This green seaweed contains a lot of iodine, giving watery kimchi a tangy taste, while making watery kimchi fresh and palatable. It is used in white kimchi and radish watery kimchi as well. There are three kinds of glue plant used in kimchi: dried, soaked and fresh. Dried glue plant is best when it is fresh and dark green in color, with fat branches but no foreign matter on it whatsoever. Soaked glue plant is the least frequently used of the three when making kimchi.

Chinese Chive *(buchu)*

Favored for its distinct scent, Chinese chive prevents food poisoning during the summer and helps digestion. The medium length Chinese chive tastes better than the longer one. Fresh green Chinese chive should be used when making kimchi. Avoid using dry or broken *buchu*-leek leaves. Used to make Chinese chive kimchi, it is also the main ingredient in stuffed cucumber kimchi and whole Chinese cabbage kimchi in summer.

Cucumber

The cucumber is abundant in vitamin C and minerals, which help eliminate body waste and therefore are good for skin cleansing, thus making one feel light.

The straight and vivid green cucumber with an equal thickness all the way down is best. The outer skin should be hard, but its thorn sharp. Its peduncle should not be overly dry. The cucumber with these features tastes juicy and fresh.

Eggplant

A summer produce, the ideal eggplant should be smooth, purple, lustrous and bear no scars on the surface skin. The outer skin should be thin, whereas its meat should be soft but tight. Its seed should not be fully grown. Avoid eggplants with an overly dry peduncle. Also, the straighter its shape, the better. Preserve it at room temperature rather than at a cool temperature.

Lanceolate (*deodeok*)

Besides its strong scent and bitter and sweet tastes that stimulate any appetite, the lanceolate is loved for its ability to rejuvenate and lower high blood pressure, strengthen the lungs and diminish the effects of arthritis. Choose a straight and medium sized lanceolate with fewer fine side roots. It is not easy to peel off its outer crust. So, in order to do this effectively, emerse it in water until its crust becomes soft, or boil it lightly and then peel off the outer skin with a small chopping knife or peeler.

Korean Pear (*bae*)

The Korean pear, otherwise known as *bae*, is sweet and juicy. It is used mainly for making watery kimchi, wrapped-up kimchi or fusion kimchi. It tenderizes beef and so is used when seasoning beef for barbecue *bulgogi*, or presented as dessert after a beef dish has been served. It is an excellent way to treat throat irritations. The Korean pear that is produced around Naju, North Jeolla province is especially delicious and therefore highly valued for its sweet, juicy and refreshing characteristics.

Pine nut

The pine nut is widely used in Korean cuisine. It is used in watery kimchi and wrapped-up kimchi, and is also used in fusion kimchi for those who are not used to eating spicy kimchi.

Pimento/Sweet Pepper

The pimento is a type of pepper, but one that is not hot. It is known to strengthen digestive tracts and lesson the hardening of the arteries and hypertension. Choose a lustrous and well-formed pimento with thick skin and without spots or scars on it. There should be few seeds inside and the peduncle should not be dehydrated. Wipe off any moisture on its skin, as moisture tends to spoil it. To preserve a pimento, put it in a vinyl bag and keep it in the refrigerator.

Cauliflower

Loved for its unique taste, the firm, white and round cauliflower is abundant in vitamin C and calcium. Be careful of any cauliflower that is yellowish in appearance, for that means it is most likely spoiled. The best cauliflower will be heavy and about 15 cm in diameter. To preserve it properly, dehydrate it a little and keep it in the refrigerator.

Asparagus

A young, soft and thick asparagus stem is good for chewing, and is also good for the kidneys, assisting in the urination process. Choose a soft and lustrous asparagus with fresh green leaves, and avoid those with fuzz along their sides. Asparagus whose top petals are flocked together in the shape of a flower are best. There are two kinds of edible asparagus: yellow and white. The former is more fragrant and nutritious than the latter. Since fresh asparagus spoils easily, it is often boiled for 2-5 minutes immediately after being harvested, before it is frozen or canned in 5% brine.

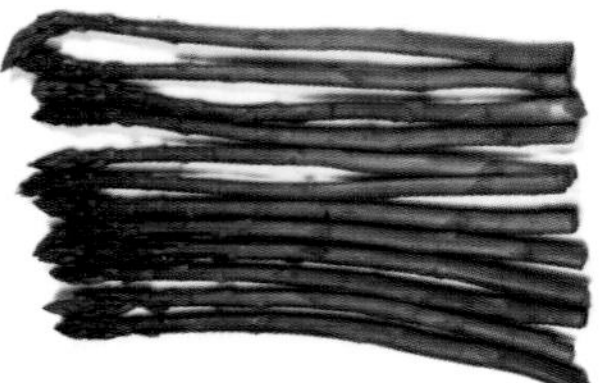

Cabbage

Abundant in calcium, cabbage, for all its alkaline features, is good for normalizing gastritis and relieving constipation, especially when it is boiled. Since it lowers high blood pressure and reduces sugar contents in blood, it is an excellent food for those people suffering from diabetes and/or hypertension. Make sure to choose one with clean, fresh, lustrous and green outer leaves. Rather than one with a large head, a heavier one with a flat head and with an unprotruded lower portion close to the root is better. When the outer leaves are hard to tear off, the cabbage is of good quality. When storing, wrap it in plastic and place it into the refrigerator, or wrap it in paper and keep it in a cool place at less than 5℃.

Broccoli

Exuding sweetness, broccoli prevents people from aging and abounds in vitamins A and C. A lustrous, dense and green head of broccoli with short stems and with fresh cross sections cut across it is best. The head of broccoli should be small and dense. Avoid broccoli with blooms or with split stems, or when it is yellow or light brown.

Rucola

Rucola, a bitter and hot vegetable, is also known as rocket, roquette, and rugula. It is popular in Italian cuisine. It abounds in vitamins A and C, and is good for digestion and colds. Rucola with clean thick green leaves and a fresh, elastic but somewhat hard stem is best. To store properly, wash, drain and place in an air-tight container before putting it in the refrigerator. It is best consumed within two days.

Celery

The characteristic flavor of celery eliminates the peculiar smell of meat, so it is recommended to have them together. Celery stimulates stomach functions, strengthening it, and relieves fatigue. Its stem to the first knot, 20-25 cm long, should be light green, thick and soft. Long, green, lustrous celery whose cross-section is like a half moon and does not show any sign of browning is best. When bent, the stem should be elastic; otherwise, it is spoiled. When preserving it in the refrigerator, do not fold or otherwise bend it.

Carrot

The carrot abounds in carotin and iron and is excellent for those who have trouble seeing in the dark. The entire root should be thick—almost the same thickness from head to tail. Its surface should be smooth, lustrous and fresh. When all these conditions are met, the carrot is soft and contains no hard wick on it. It can be stored in the refrigerator, but if it is watery, wash and put it into a plastic bag before placing it in the refrigerator. Since the carrot is hard, it can be preserved longer.

Green Bean

This sweet green bean is good for the kidneys. It stimulates the flow of urine and is excellent for those with diabetes. Fresh, firm, bright green beans without any scratches on them are best. The pod should be small, not dry, and without any furrow line. Fresh green beans are soft enough to eat without cooking. Wrap it in paper when storing it in the refrigerator, and wash before cooking.

Turnip Radish

Turnip radish contains digestive agents and is sweeter than the radish. A fresh, green, firm, medium sized one that is not too dry tastes best. Avoid choosing one which is in any way torn or full of insect bites.

Endive/Chicory

Called endive in Korea and France and chicory in America and Japan, this herb is a touch bitter, with hard outer leaves. Endive that have soft outer leaves are not fresh. When it is exposed to light, its yellow color turns to purple, which indicates it has gone bad. Preserve it in the refrigerator after wrapping it in plastic.

Yacon

Yacon looks like the sweet potato and is, in fact, sweet. It is crunchy like a Korean pear and contains 86-90 percent moisture, which is why it tastes so fresh. It abounds in fiber and oligosaccharide, so is excellent for those with diabetes as well as people who are trying to lose weight. The inner leaves of the yacon are white before it fully ripens. When ripened, they turn yellow, and its outer skin becomes dry. This is when yacon tastes best. Make sure to choose yacon that is long but soft, but not large.

Chicon

Chicon is also referred to as treviso because it is grown abundantly in Treviso, Italy. It is characterized by its bitter taste and crunchiness. The bitter element intybin helps digestion. It also helps strengthen blood vessels. The best chicon has fresh leaves and is reddish brown or distinctively purple in color.

Green Vitamin

The green vitamin, with its thick, elastic, lustrous, small green leaves abounds in vitamins and carotin, and therefore is good for one's vision. It goes well with any kind of food.

Indian Mustard Leaf

Indian mustard leaf is rich in vitamins A and C. There are actually two kinds: red and green. The thicker the color, the stronger the scent. The red one is stronger in scent and used in making kimchi with red pepper powder, whereas the green one is used in radish watery kimchi or whole Chinese cabbage white kimchi. Indian mustard leaf that is soft, shiny, fresh and about 20 cm long are generally favored.

Red Pepper

With is hot, spicy taste, red peppers stimulate the appetite and secrete digestive agents in the stomach. Korean red peppers are generally less hot than tropical ones. A good red pepper is shiny and dark crimson in color. Choose red peppers with a thick skin, and whose peduncle is tightly attached to the skin. Cut it lengthwise to see whether its seeds and seed holder are damaged by any bacteria. Red peppers with a dark reddish seed holder are preferred to those with a yellow one. Its hot and bitter taste should be well-balanced with its mild sweetness. Red pepper is dried in the sun and cut lengthwise to remove its seeds. It is then pounded and preserved in the refrigerator, later to be used mainly in kimchi.

Dried red pepper is pounded into three types of powder: fine, medium and coarse. Fine red pepper is used in watery kimchi, while medium red pepper powder is used in regular kimchi. Coarse red pepper powder is used in cooking. Dried red pepper is also sliced thin for use in making watery kimchi or when cooking other food. On the other hand, fresh red pepper can be made into a juice by blending it and then using it in kimchi. This juice gives kimchi a better taste than dried red pepper power, and helps it ferment quicker. The hottest fresh red pepper is pickled in a 5 percent salt solution. When it becomes yellowish, it is used to make radish watery kimchi.

Salt

There are two kinds of salt: crude and fine. To pickle the Chinese cabbage and radish and also salt the top of the kimchi stack, rough-grained crude salt is used; to salt the seasonings used in kimchi, fine salt is used. Dry salt, or that with the least amount of moisture and with even-sized grains, is preferred. Crude salt is blackish, while fine salt is whitish. Stone salt from a mine is bitter and therefore less favored when making kimchi than processed salt made from sun-dried sea salt.

Garlic

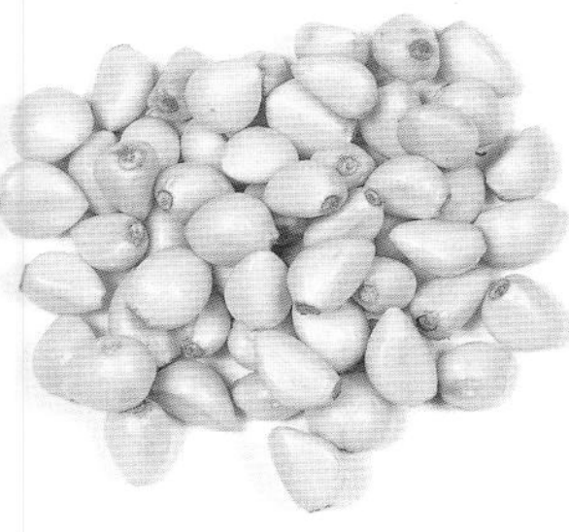

Stimulating the body's metabolism, garlic is hot and has a pungent scent and taste. Garlic which is medium sized, sufficiently dried, hard, crunchy and whose head has 6 cloves is of good quality. Each clove should have blue strips on its clear tissue on the reddish inner crust, indicating it has sufficient moisture and cannot easily be peeled off. The bigger the garlic, the less scent it has and the softer it is, making it less favored. For *gimjang* kimchi, hard garlic is best. Garlic that is cultivated in a dry field is hard, whereas garlic grown on wet land is soft. Minced garlic is usually used in kimchi. However, garlic slices are used in wrapped-up kimchi, soy sauce kimchi and thin-sliced radish and Chinese cabbage kimchi.

Ginger

Ginger, along with green onion and garlic, has a bitter taste, which helps stimulate the appetite. Ginger which is hard and yellow, with a smooth surface and large cloves, is best. Ginger with a thin, clean and moist skin, and with less fiber in it tastes very strong, making it the desired type of ginger. There are three different types of ginger that can be processed: minced ginger, used in radish kimchi, *kkakdugi*, and ordinary kimchi; finely-filtered juicy ginger, used in soy sauce kimchi and thin-sliced radish and Chinese cabbage kimchi, *nabak* kimchi; and thin-sliced ginger, used in *dongchimi* and radish watery kimchi.

Oyster

Nicknamed the milk of the sea because it abounds in calcium and iron, oysters give a clean taste to kimchi. Larger and clear colored oysters are best. Wash all oysters in brine by shaking them, taking care that they don't break or get crushed. Oysters are only used in kimchi that will be consumed within a month of making it.

Pickled Baby Shrimp

Pickled baby shrimp caught during June of the lunar calendar are best for kimchi. They are generally fermented for 2-3 months in a cool place like a cave. Those which are clean and clear in shape, pinkish in color and larger and fatter in size are of the best quality. Baby shrimp juice, when pickled, is usually whitish and creamy and has less of a fishy smell. It is used more than any other pickled fish or pickled fish juice when making kimchi .

Salted Anchovy

Salted anchovy is the most common pickled fish along with pickled baby shrimp, and tastes savory and sweet. Anchovy caught in May or June is fat and is optimal for pickling. Well salted anchovy with in discernable bones and a sweet–not fishy–smell are best. Dark, reddish anchovy are best for kimchi.

6. Kimchi Utensils

Traditional Kimchi Utensils

Chopping Board (*doma*)

Made of thick, hard wood.

Knife (*kal*)

Used to cut kimchi ingredients such as Chinese cabbage, radish, green onion, Indian mustard leaf, and cucumber.

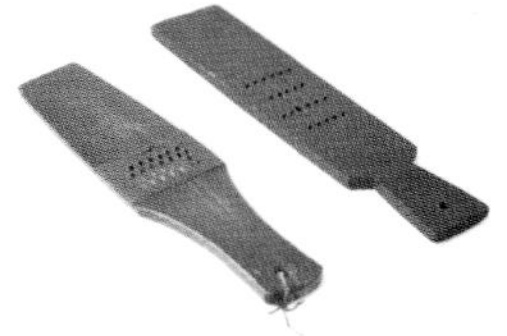

Chopping Knife (*chaekal*)

Used for chopping large amounts of radishes in a short period of time.

Modern-day Kimchi Utensils

Chopping board (*doma*)

Used for chopping Chinese cabbage and radish, it has become thinner and smaller over the years. Besides the wood chopping board, some are now made with synthetic materials.

Knife (*kal*)

Used for cutting Chinese cabbage, radish and other kimchi ingredients, the modern knife is made of stainless steel, rather than wrought iron.

Chopping Knife (*chaekal*)

Used to chop large amounts of vegetables far more conveniently than an ordinary kitchen knife.

Traditional Kimchi Utensils

Mortar Bowl (*hwak*)

Used to grind seasoning ingredients like red pepper, garlic, ginger and salt.

Grinding Porcelain (*hwakdok*)

Used to grind grains or seasonings by rolling or moving it from side to side.

Grater (*gangpan*)

Used for grating or juicing vegetables. A must-have in very kitchen.

Porcelain Saucer (*soraegi*)

Large porcelain saucer without a supporting ring under it used to wash or hold vegetables.

Deep Round Pottery Bowl (*jabaegi*)

A blackish brown pottery bowl used to wash or pickle vegetables.

Large Wooden Bowl (*hamjibak*)

Used when mixing seasonings or mixing the radish cubes with seasonings.

Present-day Kimchi Utensils

Blender (*honhapgi*)

Used to grind seasoning ingredients such as garlic, ginger and onion.

Large Bowl (*bol*)

Used when washing or pickling vegetables, or mixing vegetables with seasonings.

Airtight Container (*milpyeyonggi*)

Seasoned fresh kimchi is put snugly into this kind of container to remove any excess air from the kimchi. Air can be partially removed through the cover before putting it into the refrigerator for longer preservation.

Kimchi Fridge (*dimchae*)

Widely used in Korea today, this can ferment fresh kimchi at the optimal temperature so that seasonings can permeate thoroughly into the main kimchi ingredients. This helps preserve kimchi longer without its taste being spoiled.

Traditional Kimchi Utensils

Basket (*sokuri*)

Used for storing salt or draining water from Chinese cabbage that is pickled and washed, this round knitted basket is made with either willow twigs or thinly-sliced bamboo.

Flat Basket (*chaeban*)

Usually made from bush clover or bamboo strips, it is used to drain or dry water from the Chinese cabbage after pickling and washing it.

Pickle Crock (*jeotgal hangari*)

Unlike other crocks that are potbellied, this is flat, and used for storing pickled seafood.

Kimchi Crock (kimchi *hangari*)

Kimchi stored in a kimchi pottery crock is done so for a longer period of time. There are regional varieties that differ in form and size.

Double Decker Crock (*ijungdok*)

A double decker crock is used for preserving kimchi for a longer period of time during the summer by placing it in a stream where cool mountain water flows. When water flows along the upper deck and also by the side of the lower one, kimchi is kept fresher for longer than usual.

Traditional Kimchi Utensils

Potbelly Vessel (*bosigi*)

The potbelly kimchi crock is tall but its middle portion is far larger than its mouth.

Persimmon Crock (*gam hangari*)

Because its mouth is small like the surface of a persimmon, kimchi stored in a persimmon crock can be protected from exposure to air, which can otherwise lead to kimchi turning rancid.

Wooden Kimchi Crock (*namu* kimchi *dok*)

In mountainous areas where pottery jars were traditionally not in abundant supply, a wooden kimchi crock was used instead.

Kimchi Storage Hut (kimchi *gwang*)

A makeshift *gimjang* kimchi storage device used during the winter to preserve kimchi longer and protect it from wind and snow.

7. Kimchi: More Than Just a Side Dish

Kimchi has long been one of the most important food items for Koreans, especially between the late winter and the early spring when fresh vegetables were not easily available in the past. As a result, a large amount of kimchi, called *gimjang* kimchi, was made traditionally at each household in the late autumn or early winter. *Gimjang* kimchi has historically been made on or around November 7 in rural areas, the onset of winter, and a little later in urban areas.

In late autumn, when many people are preparing to make *gimjang* kimchi, temporary *gimjang* markets are set up where large amounts of *gimjang* kimchi ingredients are brought in to be sold to the public. This includes the main ingredients in kimchi–Chinese cabbage and radish–as well as all the seasoning materials, such as Welsh onions, green onions, watercress, Indian mustard leaves, ginger, and chestnuts.

In the past, when Koreans lived with many extended family members, about 70-100 heads of cabbage (each approximately 2 kg each) were made into *gimjang* kimchi per household. However, with the advent of the nuclear family, this number has decreased to 20-25 heads of cabbage and 10-15 radishes for a household of five family members. Furthermore, it is becoming more common for people to buy commercially made kimchi all year round.

The process by which kimchi is made is a very social one, usually bringing together friends, neighbors and relations. While making kimchi, women–for they are invariably the ones making it–can exchange information on different methods to make kimchi as they enjoy the festive atmosphere.

Cabbage Market
Huge piles of Chinese cabbage on sale.

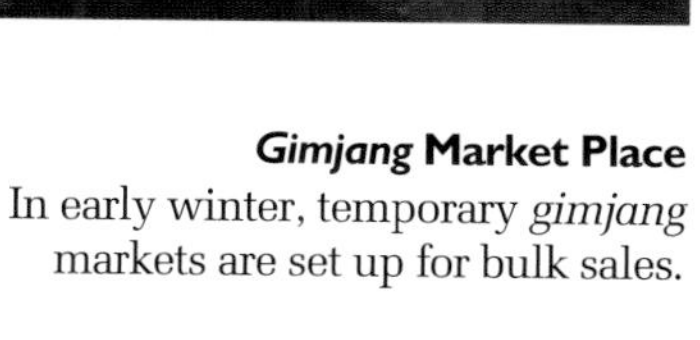

***Gimjang* Market Place**
In early winter, temporary *gimjang* markets are set up for bulk sales.

***Gimjang* Gathering**
Gimjang kimchi being made by volunteers in Insa-dong for needy neighbors.

1. Whole Chinese Cabbage Kimchi (*Tong Baechu* Kimchi)
2. Seasoned Fresh Chinese Cabbage Kimchi (*Baechu Geotjeori*)
3. White Kimchi (*Baek* Kimchi)
4. White Wrapped-up Kimchi (*Baek Bossam* Kimchi)
5. Chopped Kimchi (*Nabak* Kimchi)
6. Sweet Whole Chinese Cabbage Kimchi (*Banji/Baekji*)
7. Soy Sauce Kimchi (*Jang* Kimchi)
8. Cube Radish Kimchi (*Kkakdugi*)
9. Cube Oyster Radish Kimchi (*Gul Kkakdugi*)
10. Watery Radish Kimchi (*Dongchimi*)
11. Scaly Kimchi (*Bineul Kimchi*)
12. Obliquely Sliced Radish Kimchi (*Bijimi*)
13. Radish Strip Kimchi (*Chae* Kimchi)
14. Young Radish Kimchi (*Yeolmu* Kimchi)
15. Young Radish Watery Kimchi (*Yeolmu Mul* Kimchi)
16. Stuffed Cucumber Kimchi (*Oi Sobagi*)
17. Cucumber Watery Kimchi (*Oi Mul* Kimchi)
18. Sliced Ginseng Kimchi (*Susam Nabak* Kimchi)
19. Tangerine Watery Kimchi (*Gyul Mul* Kimchi)
20. Lanceolate Kimchi (*Deodeok* Kimchi)

Whole Chinese Cabbage Kimchi

TONG BAECHU KIMCHI

A combination of Chinese cabbage and radishes with seafood and various seasonings and spices, whole cabbage kimchi is abundant in various nutrients and favored for its refreshing, clean and palatable taste. In the past, it was made for the winter when fresh vegetables were scarce. Whole cabbage kimchi tastes better during the winter, but is now available at any time throughout the year.

INGREDIENTS

14 kg (7 heads) Chinese cabbage
1,120 g (7 cups) coarse salt
7 *l* (35 cups) water, 4.5 kg (3 ea) radishes
1.5 kg Welsh onion, 50 g glue plant
400 g Indian mustard leaf
800 g watercress
600 g threaded green onion
350 g (7 heads) minced garlic
170 g minced ginger
450 g (2 cups) salted anchovy juice
250g (1 cup) pickled baby shrimp juice
400 g (2 cups) fresh oysters
200 g (1 cup) fresh shrimp
320 g (4 cups) red pepper powder
210 g (1 cup) fine salt, 80 g (1/2 cup) sugar

TIPS

* The taste of Chinese cabbage kimchi depends very much upon its seasonings and also on the degree of pickling. Be sure to pickle the cabbage in brine solution to help it retain its own moisture. Avoid spraying salt directly over the fresh cabbage.
* Avoid pickling the cabbage for longer than 6-8 hours in the brine, especially at a lower temperature, because the nutrients of the cabbage, such as sugar, amino acid and vitamin C, will be dissolved into the brine and lost.
* Store the stuffed cabbage in several small crocks rather than in a single large one, to maintain its freshness, thus keeping the kimchi near the bottom of the crock from becoming too salty.

DIRECTIONS

1 Remove the coarse outer Chinese cabbage leaves and save them for later use. Cut each cabbage lengthwise into two halves from the root to the middle, and tear them apart completely with your hands. Pickle them for 6-8 hours in a 15% coarse salt solution. Wash them and drain.

2 Cut the radishes into thin and narrow stripes about 4 cm long. Cut the Indian mustard leaf, threaded green onion and watercress at 4 cm intervals. Cut the large green onion into 4 cm intervals and then thinly slice them.

3 Scoop and mince the pickled baby shrimp. Wash the oysters and shrimp in brine and drain. Soak the red pepper powder in the salted anchovy juice.

4 Coat the radish strips with the soaked red pepper powder in the shrimp juice, and then add all the other seasonings to them, mixing everything together thoroughly. Put the oysters and shrimp into the entire mix, flavoring with sugar and salt, to make the stuffing. (Photos 1 & 2)

5 Put the stuffing between the leaves of cabbage from the center, coating the entire surface of each leaf with the stuffing. Band the stuffed cabbage with its coarse outer leaves. Put the cabbages into the crock, filling up 70-80% of its total capacity. (Photos 3 & 4)

6 Cover the entire stack with coarse outer cabbage leaves, lest the stack is exposed to air. For longer preservation, spray fine salt over them while stacking them.

* This kimchi should be kept at about 20℃ for 3~4 days to reach proper fermentation.
* In the summer, it is recommended to add *buchu*-leek to it for longer preservation and the prevention of harmful bacteria.
* To make fried rice with kimchi, first squeeze off kimchi juice, then chop the kimchi and fry it in an oiled frying pan. Add cooked rice to it by mixing.

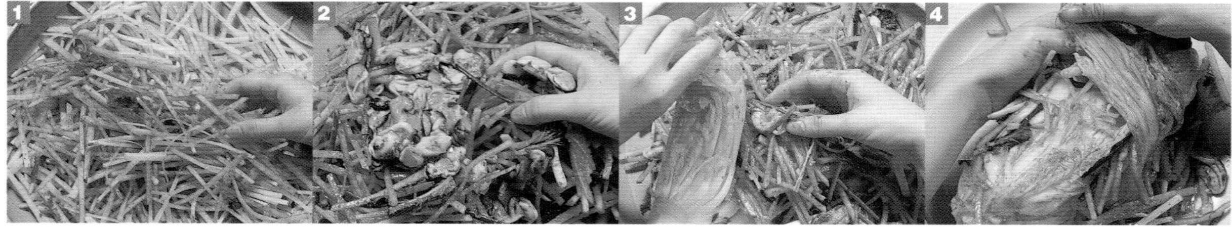

Seasoned Fresh Chinese Cabbage Kimchi
Baechu Geotjeori

This kimchi is made with a small amount of pickled baby shrimp and other seasonings, not unlike a salad. In order to ensure the fresh taste and fragrance of the Chinese cabbage, this type of kimchi can be eaten immediately, before fermentation.

Ingredients

1 kg (1/2 head) Chinese cabbage
80 g (1/2 cup) coarse salt
60 g (4 ea) fresh red peppers
40 g (1/2 cup) red pepper powder
25 g (1/2 head) minced garlic
15 g minced ginger
40 g (2 Tss) pickled baby shrimp
10 g (2 Tss) sesame oil
2 Tss sesame oil, 30 g (2 Tss) sugar
240 g (3 stalks) Welsh onion
20 g threaded green onion
5 g (1 ts) fine salt

Tips

* Add sesame oil just before serving, so the original taste of the Chinese cabbage can be combined with sesame oil to heighten its flavor.
* Use salt only when pickled baby shrimp is not available or not desired.
* This kimchi goes well with boiled or broiled pork.

Directions

1 Cut the Chinese cabbage into two halves lengthwise, pickle lightly, and wash and drain. Tear the cabbage leaves and cut them into small bite-size pieces. (Photo 1)

2 Drain the pickled baby shrimp, mince minutely and put it back into its juice. Cut each fresh red pepper into two halves lengthwise, removing all seeds. Slice them into 2-3 cm long strips. Cut the threaded green onion into 3-4 cm lengths. (Photo 2)

3 Thinly slice the Welsh onion.

4 Soak the red pepper powder in the pickled baby shrimp. Add to it the minced garlic, minced ginger, minced pickled baby shrimp, sliced Welsh onion, threaded green onion, fried whole sesame and red pepper powder, mixing them together to make the seasoning mix. (Photo 3)

5 Coat the soused cabbage with the seasoning mix, adding sugar and sesame oil to taste. To be eaten at once. (Photo 4)

White Kimchi
Baek Kimchi

In place of red pepper powder, various ingredients and seasonings are used, whereby the white kimchi becomes rich in juice and tastes very fresh.

Ingredients

4 kg (2 heads) Chinese cabbage
320 g (2 cups) coarse salt
2 *l* (10 cups) water
500 g (1/2 ea) radish, 50 g watercress
50 g threaded green onion
50 g Indian mustard leaf
500 g (1 ea) Korean pear (*bae*)
200 g (8 ea) chestnuts
20 g (5 ea) dried jujubes
16 g (4 ea) *pyogo* mushrooms (shiitake)
5 g (5 ea) stone mushrooms
480 g (6 stalks) Welsh onion
50 g (1 head) minced garlic
25 g minced ginger, 4 g threaded red pepper
100 g pickled corvenia
20 g (2 Tss) pine nuts, 15 g (1 Ts) fine salt

Tips

* Since it is not a hot dish, this is loved by many who do not enjoy spicy kimchi.
* Leave the kimchi for up to four days at room temperature, lower than 18℃, to ensure complete fermentation, as the kimchi juice is somewhat salty.
* Slice the chestnuts, jujubes, *pyogo* and stone mushrooms into thin strips to make the kimchi look elaborate.
* Because white kimchi is less salty, its taste deteriorates quickly. Be sure to cover the kimchi stack with the coarse outer leaves to prevent any from air getting in.
* Stone mushrooms grow on rocks. They should be soaked in boiled water, at which time the center supporting stem can be removed.

Directions

1. Cut each Chinese cabbage lengthwise into two halves and pickle them in a 15% coarse salt solution for 6-8 hours Wash and drain. Cut off and discard any remaining roots from the cabbage.
2. Slice the radish into thin strips about 4 cm long and pickle. Cut the watercress, threaded green onion and Indian mustard leaf into 3-4 cm lengths. Slice the pickled corvenia into thin pieces. (Photo 1)
3. Peel the Korean pear and the chestnuts, then slice their contents into thin strips about 3 cm long. Peel off the outer crust and meat of each jujube into a single strip, and then cut it into thin strips. Soak and cut the *pyogo* and stone mushrooms into strips.
4. Cut the Welsh onion, garlic and ginger into thin strips. Cut threaded red pepper into 2-3 cm long pieces.
5. Mix in all the seasonings to make the stuffing, adding salt if necessary. (Photo 2)
6. Insert the stuffing between the leaves and bind each stuffed cabbage with its outer leaves, lest the stuffing should fall out. Then stack the stuffed cabbage tightly in a crock. Boil the leftover pickled corvenia to extract its juice. Make mildly salty kimchi juice with the boiled corvenia juice and pour it into the crock, until the stack is submerged. Cover the kimchi stack with the salted coarse outer leaves of the cabbage to block the exposure of air to the kimchi. (Photos 3 & 4)
7. Fermentation may take two weeks around the time of *gimjang* in early November.

White Wrapped-up Kimchi
Baek Bossam Kimchi

This special kimchi contains pickled Chinese cabbage, radish and several delicacies, including pine nuts and chestnuts. With various seasonings added to it, this is a specialty of Kaeseong and Seoul.

Ingredients

6 kg (3 heads) Chinese cabbage
480 g (3 cups) coarse salt
1 kg (1 ea) radish
250 g (10 ea) chestnuts
500 g (1 ea) Korean pear (*bae*)
2 ea hard persimmons, 50 g (10 ea) jujubes
150 g Indian mustard leaf
50 g watercress
100 g threaded green onion
4 g thereded red pepper
100 g (2 heads) minced garlic
20 g (2 pieces) minced ginger
20 g (5 ea) *pyogo* mushrooms
5 g (5 ea) stone mushrooms
250 g (1 cup) pickled baby shrimp
24 g (3 Tss) pine nuts
150 g (1 ea) octopus, 15 g (1 Ts) fine salt

Tips

* Choose the larger Chinese cabbage leaves.
* This white wrapped-up kimchi becomes sour soon, so make a small quantity of it at a time.
* Wrapped-up kimchi is the same as this kimchi except for the fact that wrapped-up kimchi has red pepper powder and a larger amount of kimchi juice.

Directions

1 Cut each Chinese cabbage into two halves lengthwise. Cut the radish into halves lengthwise, too. Pickle them in 15% brine for 6-8 hours, wash and drain.

2 Chop the cabbage into 3 cm long pieces and the radish into 2 cm × 2 cm × 0.5 cm pieces. (Photo 1)

3 Thinly slice the chestnuts. Peel off the crust and meat of each dried jujube into a single wide strip, and then thinly slice it. Trim the pine nuts. Chop the sliced threaded red pepper into 3 cm long pieces. Scoop pickled baby shrimp from the juice and chop them up into small pieces. Chop the Welsh onion, Indian mustard leaf and watercress at 2 cm intervals. Soak the *pyogo* mushroom and thinly slice. Then do the same with the stone mushroom. (Photo 2)

4 Scatter salt over the octopus and rub it with your hands, drain and cut it into 2 cm long pieces. Mix the squid with other seasonings to make a mix. Adjust for taste with fine salt. (Photo 3)

5 Spread 3 or 4 large leaves of the cabbage in a bowl. Place the chopped cabbage over them, then place the mix in the center. Cover the mix with the cabbage leaves, overlapping their ends in the middle over top so that you make a bundle. Place each wrapped-up cabbage bundle in the chosen crock tightly, covering the stack with the outer leaves of the cabbage. Make a sufficient amount of mildly salty seasoning juice, and pour it into the crock. (Photos 4 & 5)

Chopped Kimchi
Nabak Kimchi

A very watery dish, chopped kimchi is composed of sliced radish as well as chopped Chinese cabbage and other seasonings, giving it a clean, fresh taste. It can be made easily all year round.

Ingredients

500 g (1/4 head) Chinese cabbage
400 g (1/3 head) radish
160 g (2 stalks) Wakegi green onion
25 g (1/2 head) minced garlic
15 g minced ginger
30 g (2 ea) fresh red pepper
50 g watercress
30 g (5 Tss) red pepper powder
3 g (1 ts) pine nuts
45 g (3 Tss) coarse salt
2 *l* kimchi juice [2 *l* (10 cups) water + 50 g (1/3 cup) fine salt]

Tips

* To make crunchy chopped kimchi, salting is done twice, first for pickling and then for fermenting after the final mixing of vegetables with seasonings. The Chinese cabbage is pickled before the radish.
* For immediate consumption, boil and cool the kimchi juice, then pour it into the kimchi crock little by little.
* To make this particular kimchi look better, either cucumber or carrot may be added. However, the ascorbinase enzyme in the carrot tends to destroy all vitamin C in kimchi, so adding only a small portion of carrot is recommended. As a substitute for the carrot, fresh red pepper may be used.
* This popular watery kimchi goes well with rice cake, *tteok,* and porridge.

Directions

1 Chop the soft inner leaves of the Chinese cabbage and the radish into thin pieces (2.5 cm × 3 cm), then pickle them in a 15% coarse salt solution and drain. (Photo 1 & 2)

2 Cut the Wakegi green onion, garlic and ginger into 3 cm long thin pieces. Cut the fresh red pepper into two halves lengthwise, removing all seeds as you do so. Slice them into 3 cm long pieces, too.

3 Mix the cabbage and radish with the Wakegi green onion, garlic, ginger and fresh red pepper. Put the entire mix into a crock. (Photo 3)

4 Using the brine already used for pickling the cabbage and radish, make kimchi juice by wrapping the red pepper powder in a dry cloth with tiny holes in it, shaking it in the brine, and then adjusting the taste with fine salt. Finally, pour the juice into the crock. (Photo 4 & 5)

5 When this kimchi is fermented and ready to serve, put the watercress over the vegetables and float the well-trimmed pine nuts over the kimchi juice.

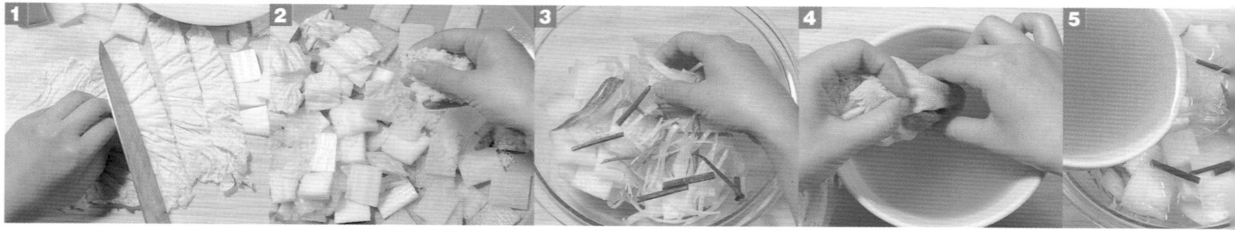

Sweet Whole Chinese Cabbage Kimchi
Banji/Baekji

To make *banji* kimchi, seasonings are inserted between the Chinese cabbage leaves before the stuffed cabbage is bound by its outer leaves. Salted anchovy juice is mixed with honey or sugar and then poured into the cabbage stack of *banji* kimchi.

Ingredients

1 kg (1/2 head) Chinese cabbage
80 g (1/2 cup) coarse salt
400 g radish, 250 g (1/2 ea) apple
250 g (1/2 ea) Korean pear (*bae*)
50 g (2 ea) chestnuts
20 g (5 ea) jujubes, 5 g pine nuts
80 g (1 stalk) threaded green onion
50 g (1 head) garlic, 20 g ginger
100 g (1/2 cup) salted anchovy juice
20 g (2 Tss) fine salt, 8 g (1/2 Ts) sugar
1 g threaded red pepper

Tips

* *Banji* kimchi contains no red pepper powder but a lot of juice, which makes it a kind of watery kimchi.
* Cabbage contains a lot of vitamin C and calcium in it. Not very much of this is lost when making kimchi.
* When *banji* kimchi becomes sour, remove its juice by squeezing it, then mix it with poultry meat, bean curd and green bean sprouts to make dumplings.

Directions

1 Cut the Chinese cabbage lengthwise into two halves from the root to the middle and tear them apart completely. Pickle them for 6-8 hours in a 15% coarse salt solution, wash and drain.

2 Cut the radish into strips (2 cm long, 2.5 cm wide and 0.7 cm thick). Take off the shells of the chestnuts, trim and thinly slice them. Thinly slice the Welsh onion, garlic and ginger as well. (Photo 1 & 2)

3 Peel off the outer skin and meat of each jujube before thinly slicing each one. Peel off the skin of the apple and Korean pear and thinly slice them. Cut the threaded red pepper into 2 cm lengths.

4 Put all the seasonings together to make a stuffing mix. And add sugar and fine salt to it. Adjust for taste as you see fit. (Photo 3)

5 Put the stuffing mix between the leaves of the cabbage in the center. Band the stuffed cabbage with its outer leaves. Stack up the cabbages tightly in a crock. Pour kimchi juice made of residual seasonings, including salt and sugar, into the crock. Optimal fermentation is reached in two weeks. (Photo 4)

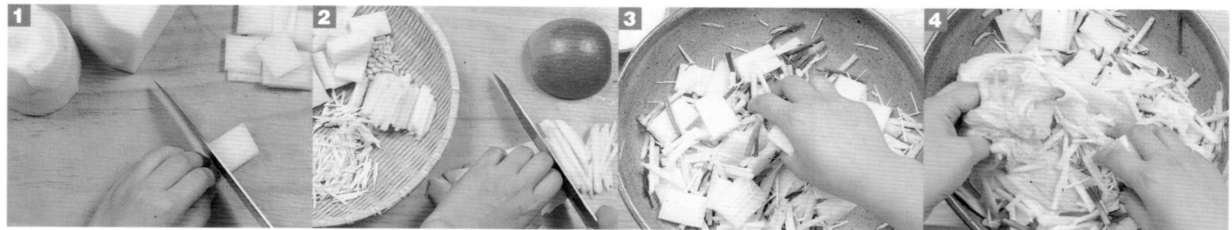

Soy Sauce Kimchi
JANG KIMCHI

This is a special kimchi dish enjoyed on special occasions such as *Seol*, Lunar New Year' s Day, and *Chuseok*, Korean Thanksgiving. To make this kimchi, the Chinese cabbage and radish are pickled, and then the Korean pear, chestnuts, *pyogo* and stone mushrooms, and pine nuts are added to make this refreshing and savory dish.

INGREDIENTS

500 g (1/2 head) inner core of Chinese cabbage
700 g (1/2 ea) radish
100 g (1/2 cup) aged soybean sauce
50 g Indian mustard leaf
20 g (4 ea) *pyogo* mushrooms
16 g (4 ea) stone mushrooms
500 g (1 ea) Korean pear (*bae*)
240 g (3 stalks) threaded green onion
50 g (1 head) minced garlic
20 g minced ginger, 100 g watercress
200 g (8 ea) chestnuts
1 g threaded red pepper
10 g (1 Ts) pine nuts
30 g (2 Tss) sugar, 0.4 *l* (2 cups) water

TIPS

* This soy sauce kimchi is distinguished for containing, as its main ingredients, the Korean pear, chestnuts, and *pyogo* mushrooms, as well as aged soybean sauce. These flavors all blend in nicely into the soybean sauce, making this kimchi mildly salty and very particular in taste.
* The sousing order is important for a better result: since the Chinese cabbage contains enough moisture of its own, it is better to souse it before the radish.
* This kimchi is more favored with rice cake, *tteok,* or with white rice cake soup rather than with ordinary cooked rice.
* Korean pear (*bae*), helps make this kimchi juice sweet and fresh.

DIRECTIONS

1 Cut the Chinese cabbage and radish into small pieces (2.5 cm × 3 cm × 0.5 cm). Pickle the cabbage with the aged soybean sauce. Add the radish to it and pickle for a further 1 to 2 hours. (Photos 1 & 2)

2 Thinly slice the chestnuts and the Korean pear. Cut the watercress and Indian mustard leaf into 3 cm lengths strips.

3 Thinly slice the *pyogo* and stone mushrooms into strips. Cut the threaded red pepper into smaller pieces 2-3 cm long.

4 Drain off the aged soybean sauce from the cabbage and radish. Add all the seasonings before mixing it all up. Stack the entire mix in a crock tightly. (Photo 3)

5 Add water to the soybean sauce, adjusting its taste with sugar and salt. Pour the liquid over the mix in the crock. Fermentation usually takes two or three days. (Photo 4)

Cube Radish Kimchi

KKAKDUGI

The radish is cut into cubes, mixed with seasonings, and enjoyed for its crunchiness.

INGREDIENTS

1.5 kg (1 ea) radish
100 g threaded green onion
100 g watercress
25 g (1 Ts) minced garlic
8 g (1 Ts) minced ginger
60 g (3 Tss) pickled baby shrimp
40 g (1/2 cup) red pepper powder
15 g (1 Ts) sugar, 45 g (3 Tss) fine salt

TIPS

* Since the autumn radish is harder and sweeter than the spring one, sugar should be added with discretion. For sweet autumn radish kimchi, less sugar is added after the seasoning mix is made, whereas for the spring radish kimchi, more sugar is added before the seasoning mix is made. During the summer, squeeze off the moisture from the radish after pickling for a better taste.
* For immediate consumption and a clear taste, fresh oysters may be added. Winter kimchi goes well with thick beef stew/soup or beef rib soup.
* Some sliced and pickled Chinese cabbage leaves may be added to this cube radish kimchi to add flavor. The leaves of the radish may be used intact with its roots.

DIRECTIONS

1 Cube the radish into 2.5 cm blocks. Cut the threaded green onion and watercress in 3 cm intervals. (Photo 1)

2 Mince the pickled baby shrimp minutely after scooping it from its juice and then put it back. (Photo 2) (Note: Mince garlic and ginger if not ready yet.)

3 Coat the cubed radishes with red pepper powder, and then add garlic, ginger, pickled baby shrimp, sugar, threaded green onion and watercress. Mix everything together and adjust taste with fine salt. (Photos 3 & 4)

4 Fill a crock tightly with the entire mix and let it ferment for two weeks.

Cube Oyster Radish Kimchi

GUL KKAKDUGI

Fresh oysters and radishes make this kimchi taste clean and refreshing. Eat it soon after it's made, as this kimchi spoils quickly.

INGREDIENTS

3 kg (2 ea) radishes
100 g threaded green onion
50 g watercress
60 g (3 Tss) pickled baby shrimp
400 g (2 cups) oysters
80 g (1 cup) red pepper powder
12 g (1/4 head) minced garlic
5 g minced ginger, 45 g (3 Tss) sugar
30 g (3 Tss) fine salt

TIPS

* When mixing the seasonings, add the oysters last in case they get crushed.
* This cube oyster radish kimchi spoils easily, so only make a little at a time.
* Choose plump oysters with a fresh and milky color. Avoid using oysters during the summer when they lay eggs and become poisonous.

DIRECTIONS

1 Cut the radish cubes (2.5 cm on each side). Cut the watercress and threaded green onion into 3 cm lengths. (Photo 1)

2 Scoop out the pickled baby shrimp, mince it and then put it back into its juice. (Photo 2)

3 Wash the oysters in a salt solution and drain. Mince the garlic and ginger if not ready yet.

4 Coat the radish cubes with red pepper powder. Combine them with the minced garlic and ginger, pickled baby shrimp, threaded green onion, watercress, and oysters. Mix everything up, adjusting the taste with fine salt and sugar. (Photo 3)

5 Put the entire mix into a crock, pressing hard in case air should get into the kimchi and spoil it, and let it ferment for 3-4 days. (Photo 4)

Watery Radish Kimchi
DONGCHIMI

Medium sized Korean radishes are pickled as a whole and then fermented with pickled chili pepper in a pre-boiled and then cooled salt liquid. It is made for the winter, tasting pungent and refreshing. It goes well with Korean rice cake, *tteok*; its juice is often used for buckwheat noodle soup.

INGREDIENTS

10 kg (10 ea) Korean radishes
240 g (1½ cups) coarse salt
5 *l* (25 cups) water (for kimchi juice)
140 g (1 cup) fine salt
500 g (1 ea) Korean pear (*bae*)
70 g (1/2 ea) pomegranate
500 g Indian mustard leaf
50 g Wakegi green onion
25 g glue plant
125 g (2½ heads) minced garlic
60 g minced ginger
50 g fermented green pepper

TIPS

* The best time of year to make *dongchimi* is around *ipdong*, which usually falls around the beginning of November.
* Fresh green peppers with their peduncle intact are fermented a month earlier until they turn yellow.
* *Dongchimi* juice may be used in wheat noodle soup or buckwheat cold noodle soup. *Dongchimi* juice goes well with rice cake, *tteok*, making it taste better and more easily digestible.
* *Dongchimi* radishes may be chopped into julienne pieces and then mixed with Welsh onion, red pepper, powdered salted sesame and sesame oil. This makes a good side dish.
* The radishes can be cut flat and covered with wheat flour and egg, and then fried to make another side dish.

DIRECTIONS

1 Trim the radishes by removing their leaves and small fine roots. Wash and stack them, spraying coarse salt over each layer. Leave them to souse for 2 days. (Photos 1 & 2)

2 Add fine salt water to the brine where radishes were soused to make the kimchi juice, adjusting its taste if necessary. Boil it and let it cool.

3 Cut both the Korean pear and pomegranate into halves. Pick up 2 or 3 roots of the Wakegi green onion, Indian mustard leaf and glue plant and bind them into a bundle. Put the minced garlic and ginger in a linen bag and bind its mouth. (Photo 3)

4 Stack the radishes in the crock. Place other seasoning ingredients, such as the pomegranate and spices, including the garlic and ginger, in the linen bag, between the layers of the radishes. Place the Indian mustard leaf over the entire stack and put a rock over it to keep it submerged when the juice is poured into the crock. Pour the kimchi juice over the stack. Make the crock airtight and leave it to ferment for 5 to 10 days. (Photo 4)

* Choose medium sized hot Korean radishes with a lot of juice. They should be hard, with their heads green and their bellies bulging.
* For the clear kimchi juice of *dongchimi*, do not cut or slice the radishes. Use a seasoning bag to put garlic and ginger into. Filter the salted water with a sieve.
* *Dongchimi* juice is tasty and refreshing in proportion to the amount of the radishes, and especially so when its crock is buried in the ground to the brim. The colder the temperature, the tastier the juice becomes. A mix of beef soup with *dongchimi* juice makes delicious buckwheat noodle soup.
* To make pickled radish, soak it until it is no longer salty, then dry it and put it into soy sauce.

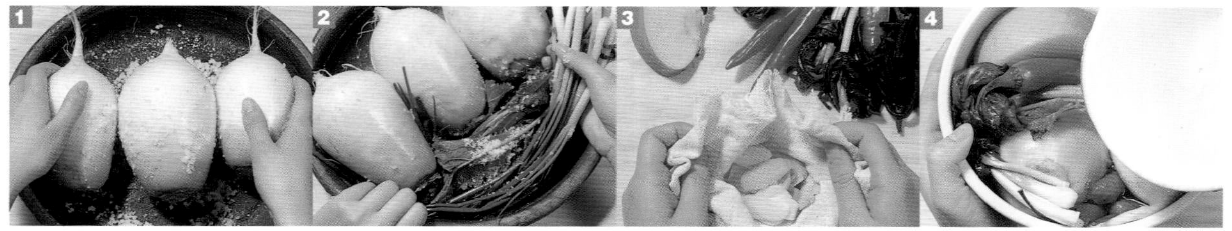

Scaly Kimchi
Bineul Kimchi

This stuffed, scaly kimchi looks similar to stuffed cucumber kimchi. For this dish, stuffing is done in the scaly slit rather than in the straight part.

Ingredients

1.6 kg (3 ea) radishes
360 g (6 leaves) Chinese cabbage
80 g (1/2 cup) coarse salt
20 g watercress
40 g threaded green onion
50 g (1 head) minced garlic
25 g minced ginger
18 g (3 Tss) red pepper powder
20 g (2 Tss) salted anchovy
10 g (1 Ts) fine salt, 0.2 l (1 cup) water

Tips

* Choose small radishes.
* Scaly radish pieces should be soused sufficiently so that putting the stuffing into the slit can be done easier. If making scaly slits on the fresh radishes is not easy, do so after sousing it.
* Scaly kimchi was usually made in the royal court, which was sometimes prepared simultaneously with cucumber scaly kimchi. Often they are stacked one layer after another, alternatively, in a crock to bring about a more refreshing taste.

Directions

1 Cut each radish into two halves. Using a knife, mark the scaly slits on one half with 3 cm intervals and pickle it in brine with the Chinese cabbage leaves. Rinse and drain the scaly radishes. (Photo 1)

2 Cut the other half of the radishes into thin strips. Add as much water as salted anchovy juice, boil and filter. (Photo 2)

3 Cut the watercress and threaded green onion into 3 cm lengths. Make the stuffing with the thin radish strips, red pepper powder, minced garlic and ginger, and salted anchovy juice by mixing them up.

4 When the radishes are well pickled, drain, then put the stuffing into the scaly radish slits. (Photo 3)

5 Rinse the cabbage leaves and drain. Apply the residual seasonings over them. Spread the cabbage leaves flat, then place the scaly and stuffed radishes over them. Wrap them all up into a bundle. Place the wrapped-up bundles into a crock, pressing down hard as you do this, and then pour 0.2 l of water on top of it. Keep the crock in a cool place for fermentation for two weeks. (Photo 4)

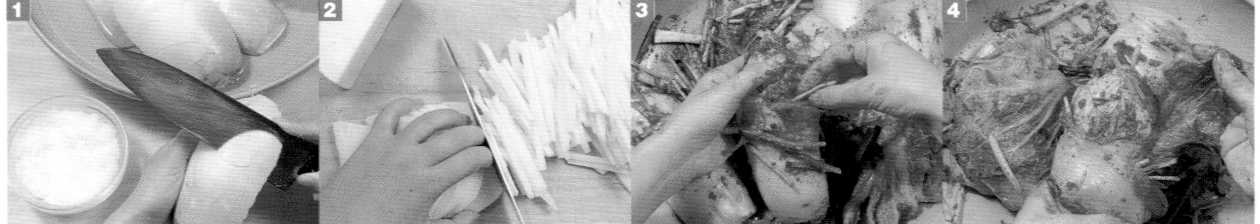

Obliquely Sliced Radish Kimchi

BIJIMI

The radish is sliced into triangular pieces and mixed with seasonings for this dish.

INGREDIENTS

2 kg (1 ea) radish, 20 g watercress
80 g (1/2 cup) coarse salt
20 g minced garlic, 10 g minced ginger
50 g threaded green onion
20 g Indian mustard leaf
40 g (1/2 cup) red pepper powder
5 g (1 ts) fine salt

TIPS

* It takes about one week for *bijimi* kimchi to ferment.
* When serving this kimchi, put watercress, Indian mustard leaf and threaded green onion on its surface to give it a better look and stir everyone's appetite.
* The Chinese cabbage and radishes are the most important vegetables in Korea. The latter contains a helpful digestive agent, diastase.

DIRECTIONS

1 Cut the radish obliquely into triangular block pieces. Pickle them lightly and drain. (Photo 1)

2 Cut the watercress into 3 cm lengths. Cut the Indian mustard leaf into smaller pieces. (Photo 2)

3 Coat the radish with red pepper powder. (Photo 3)

4 Mix the radish with the garlic, ginger, sliced threaded green onion, watercress, and Indian mustard leaf, adjusting its taste with fine salt. Put the entire mix into a crock tightly and let if ferment for one week. (Photo 4)

Radish Strip Kimchi
CHAE KIMCHI

Just before the winter, the residue of *gimjang* kimchi, mainly radish strips and various seasonings, is utilized and consumed for a short period of time before *gimjang* kimchi is fermented.

INGREDIENTS

5 kg (5 ea) radishes
500 g (1 ea) Korean pear (*bae*)
200 g (1 ea) fresh pollack
80 g (1 stalk) Welsh onion
50 g minced garlic, 20 g minced ginger
125 g (1/2 cup) pickled baby shrimp
300 g Indian mustard leaf
400 g watercress
200 g Wakegi green onion
160 g (2 cups) red pepper powder
45 g (3 Ts) sugar
140 g (1 cup) fine salt

TIPS

* A larger quantity of seafood is used in this kimchi, so it contains an abundance of protein and minerals. This is why it ferments quicker.
* This kimchi is soft and therefore suitable for older people to consume.
* This kimchi becomes sour easily, so it is recommended to make a small amount of radish strip kimchi at a time. If oysters are added, the pickling process is accelerated.

DIRECTIONS

1. Cut the radishes and the Korean pear into thin strips (5 cm long, 0.5 cm thick). (Photo 1)
2. Slice the pollack into 5 cm long, 1 cm wide pieces, then chop them again into thin strips.
3. Chop up the pickled baby shrimp after removing its juice, then put it back into its juice. Cut the watercress, Welsh onion, Wakegi green onion and Indian mustard leaf into 5 cm lengths.
4. Coat the radishes with red pepper powder. (Photo 2) Add to it the pollack and all the seasoning ingredients for mixing, adjusting its taste with sugar and fine salt. (Photos 3 & 4)
5. Place the entire mix into a crock, pressing down hard as you do this, and let it ferment for one week.

Young Radish Kimchi

YEOLMU KIMCHI

A delicacy during summer, young radish kimchi, especially its juice, renders a clean palatable taste when wheat starch is added, eliminating the pungency to its smell.

INGREDIENTS

1 kg (1 bundle) young radishes
80 g (1/2 cup) coarse salt
240 g (3 stalks) Welsh onion
50 g (1 head) minced garlic
25 g minced ginger
150 g (10 ea) fresh red peppers
10 g (1 Ts) fine salt
75 g (5 ea) fresh green peppers
0.2 *l* (1 cup) wheat starch [20 g (2 Tss) flour + 0.2 *l* (1 cup) water]

TIPS

* It takes 2-3 days for the proper fermentation of this kimchi.
* Instead of the fresh green pepper, the cucumber may be used. Since a lot of fresh red pepper juice is used (without any pickled fish juice added), young radish kimchi lasts longer in the summer with its delicate flavor, especially when kept in a cool place.
* Potato starch may be used instead of wheat flour.
* This dish goes well with barley rice or noodles.

DIRECTIONS

1 Cut the young radishes into 5 cm lengths and pickle with coarse salt. Wash and drain. (Photo 1)

2 Cut the Welsh onion into 3 cm lengths. Cut the fresh red peppers and the green peppers diagonally and remove their seeds. Grind the fresh red peppers, garlic and ginger in a blender to make the spicy seasoning mix needed for this dish.

3 Make starch with flour and water, then let it cool. Add it to the seasoning mix, adjusting taste with fine salt. (Photo 2)

4 Add young radishes, Welsh onion and fresh green pepper to the seasoning mix and then mix everything together. Put the final mix into a crock tightly. Make kimchi juice with fine salt and pour it into the crock. (Photos 3 & 4)

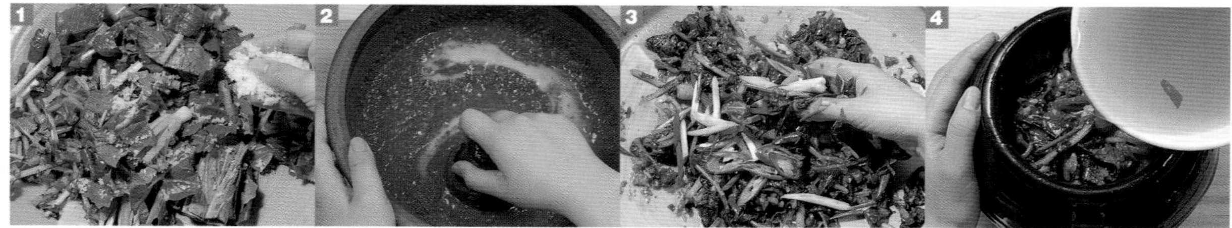

Young Radish Watery Kimchi
Yeolmu Mul Kimchi

Made with starch during the summer, this kimchi is consumed in various ways. The young radishes with their leaves are mixed with barley rice and red pepper paste to make an assorted vegetable rice dish, or its juice is used as the soup of wheat noodle or buckwheat noodles.

INGREDIENTS

400 g young radish
200 g young Chinese cabbage
30 g (2 Tss) coarse salt
25 g threaded green onion
15 g (1 ea) fresh green pepper
45 g (3 ea) fresh red peppers
25 g (1/2 head) minced garlic
15 g minced ginger
0.6 ℓ (3 cups) wheat starch [30 g (3 Tss) flour + 0.6 ℓ (3 cups) water]
10 g (1 Ts) fine salt

TIPS

* Cut the young radishes by hand rather than with a knife. Handle with care when pickling, otherwise they may become more pungent.
* When making starch over a flame, be sure to stir the watered flour slowly until the starch becomes very clear. The starch, which becomes sugar during the fermentation process in kimchi, helps its lactase to multiply, whereby the pungency of kimchi is eliminated.
* No pickled fish juice is used here, but the red pepper juice with salt is used to adjust the taste of kimchi, which is mildly salty and refreshing. Cucumber may be added to strengthen its freshness, but will make the kimchi spoil sooner.

DIRECTIONS

1 Cut the soft, fresh young radish into 4-5 cm lengths. Wash and drain, and spray salt over it for pickling. Do the same to the young Chinese cabbage. (Photo 1)
2 Cut two fresh red peppers diagonally. Cut the threaded green onion into 3-4 cm lengths.
3 Mix the diagonally-cut fresh red peppers and minced garlic and ginger in a blender to make the red pepper mix. Cut the remaining fresh red peppers and a single green pepper into strips. (Photo 2)
4 Rinse the radish and cabbage and drain. Add to them the red pepper mix, fresh red pepper and green pepper strips and threaded green onion, mixing them up. Put the entire mix into a crock tightly. (Photo 3)
5 Put the ground fresh red pepper together in a blender with wheat starch. Then add fine salt before putting in a bowl. Fermentation may take 2-3 days. (Photo 4)

* This dish goes well with cooked barley rice. They can be mixed with other seasonings and then eaten together.
*The acidized young radish kimchi may be cooked by removing its juice and then by frying it in oil.

Stuffed Cucumber Kimchi

OI SOBAGI

Soft, young cucumbers are stuffed with various seasonings after being cut lengthwise. From spring to autumn, this dish is enjoyed for its crunchiness and scent.

INGREDIENTS

600 g (4 ea) slender cucumbers
36 g (4 Tss) coarse salt
0.4 *l* (2 cups) water
12 g (2 Tss) red pepper powder
50 g (1/3 bundle) Chinese chive (*buchu*)
10 g (1 ts) minced ginger
25 g (1/2 head) minced garlic
80 g (1 stalk) Welsh onion
5 g (1 ts) fine salt

TIPS

* Choose fresh, straight, and shiny young cucumbers with no seeds. A dull, yellow or stringy cucumber will not be crunchy enough for this dish. The soused cucumber may be pressed to remove its moisture before stuffing is done; this is one way of making the cucumber crunchier.
* One of the characteristics of this stuffed cucumber dish is its clean taste. So, neither pickled fish nor its juice is used.
* Since this kimchi ferments quickly, make a small amount. Fresh stuffed cucumber can be served immediately.

DIRECTIONS

1 Rub the cucumbers with coarse salt and rinse. Cut them into 6 cm long pieces. Make lengthwise slit-cuts on each cucumber, leaving 1 cm on both ends. Pickle them for 30 minutes in a 50% coarse salt solution. (Photo 1)

2 Chop the Chinese chive and add to it the Welsh onion, garlic, ginger, red pepper powder and salt, mixing them up to make the stuffing. (Photo 2)

3 Cover the pickled cucumber in a dry linen cloth and squeeze off its moisture. Put the stuffing in the cucumber slits. (Photo 3)

4 Stack the stuffed cucumber pieces in a crock tightly. Pour water into the stuffing mix vessel and gather the residue to make kimchi juice, adjusting the taste with fine salt.

5 Pour kimchi juice into the crock until the entire cucumber stack is submerged. Place a stone or rock on the stack in case the stuffed cucumber should float to the surface of the kimchi juice. (Photo 4)

Cucumber Watery Kimchi

Oi Mul Kimchi

Cucumber watery kimchi is made of cucumber, chopped radish, Korean pear and several different seasonings, which are stuffed in its slits. This crunchy summer specialty gives off a piquant scent and flavor, and has a juice that is extremely savory.

Ingredients

500 g (3 ea) cucumbers
36 g (3 Tss) coarse salt
0.4 *l* (2 cups) water
50 g radish
125 g (1/4 ea) Korean pear (*bae*)
10 g watercress, 10 g minced garlic
5 g minced ginger
8 g (1/2 ea) fresh red pepper
10 g threaded green onion
30 g (2 Tss) fine salt, 15 g (1 Ts) sugar
1.2 *l* (6 cups) wheat starch [20 g (2 Tss) flour + 1.2 *l* (6 cups) water]

Tips

* When pickled well, the cucumber keeps its crunchiness and hardness and does not become flaccid easily.
* Cucumber kimchi turns sour easily; it is better to make a little at a time.
* The cucumber abounds in potassium, about 140mg%, which functions to remove body waste and sodium, making one feel healthier.

Directions

1. Choose fresh cucumbers that are very straight, and rub them with coarse salt. Wash and cut them into 2 cm pieces. Make lengthwise slit-cuts on each cucumber, leaving 1 cm on one end. Pickle them for 30 minutes in a 50% coarse salt solution and drain. (Photos 1 & 2)
2. Peel off the outer crust of the radish and the Korean pear and chop them into 2 cm long julienne pieces. Trim the threaded green onion and watercress and cut them at 1.5 cm intervals. Thinly slice the garlic and ginger. (Photo 3)
3. Cut the fresh red pepper into halves lengthwise. Remove its seeds and thinly slice it into julienne pieces.
4. Mix in the radish, Korean pear, threaded green onion, garlic and ginger, and then add fine salt and sugar to adjust the taste. Insert the seasonings into the cucumber slits, and stack the stuffed cucumber pieces in a container. (Photo 4)
5. Make starch with 6 cups of water and 3 table spoons of wheat flour, adjusting the taste with sugar and fine salt. Let it cool. Pour this watery starch into the kimchi container. It takes about 3-4 days for this kimchi to reach its optimal fermentation. (Photo 5)

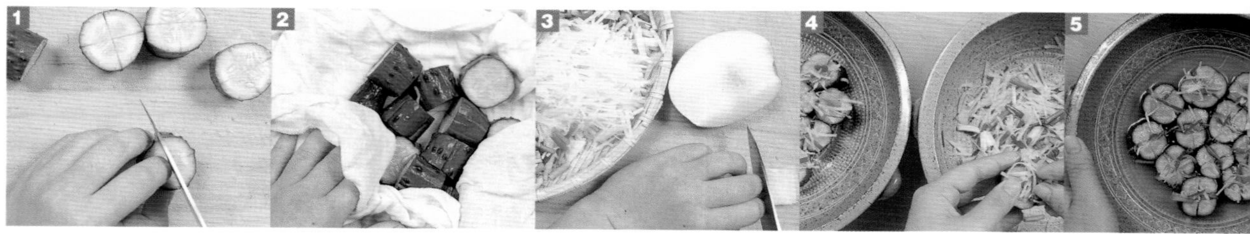

Sliced Ginseng Kimchi

Susam Nabak Kimchi

The bitter taste of ginger combines with the sweetness of the Korean pear to produce a very distinct taste in this dish.

Ingredients

1 kg fresh ginseng, 1 kg (1 ea) radish
1 kg Chinese cabbage
500 g (1 ea) Korean pear (*bae*)
125 g (5 ea) chestnuts
40 g (2½ Tss) coarse salt
30 g threaded green onion
7 g minced ginger
15 g (1/3 head) garlic
2 ℓ kimchi juice [45 g (3 Tss) fine salt + 2 ℓ (10 cups) water]

Tips

* Sugar is not usually used in this dish in order to get a cleaner taste.
* For immediate consumption, add vinegar and sugar to the fresh ginseng when pickling.
* Ginseng is known to contain large quantities of saphonin, which is good for mitigating stress, fatigue, depression, sclerosis of the heart arteries and cancer.

Directions

1 Scratch the root of the ginseng with a knife blade to remove any foreign matter, then cut it into small slices (3 cm × 1 cm × 0.5 cm). (Photo 1)

2 Cut the Chinese cabbage and radish pieces (2.5 cm × 2.5 cm × 0.5 cm). Pickle the ginseng, cabbage and radish pieces lightly with coarse salt. (Photos 2 & 3)

3 Peel off the outer crust of the Korean pear and cut it into the same size as the radish pieces. Remove the chestnut shells and slice them in the same way. Cut the threaded green onion into 3 cm long pieces. Mix in all the ingredients together.

4 Add water and fine salt to the brine used to pickle the cabbage and radish in order to make kimchi juice. Put the mix into a crock, pouring the kimchi juice over it, then wait 2-3 days for it to ferment. (Photo 4)

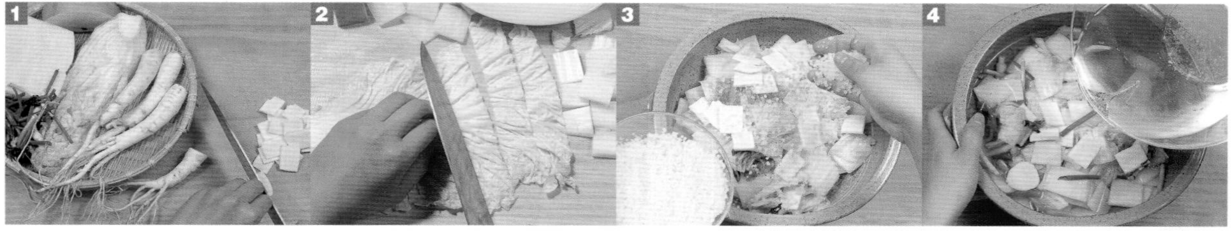

Tangerine Watery Kimchi
Gyul Mul Kimchi

Having tangerines floating in the kimchi juice of this dish is pretty, fragrant and also appetizing.

INGREDIENTS

1 kg (10 ea) tangerines
300 g (5 leaves) Chinese cabbage
300 g radish, 30 g (2 ea) fresh red peppers
24 g (2 Tss) coarse salt
50 g watercress
25 g (1/2 head) minced garlic
15 g (ginger juice 1 Ts) minced ginger
6 g (1 Ts) fine red pepper powder
30 g (2 Tss) fine salt, 5 g (1 ts) sugar
2 *l* (10 cups) water

TIPS

* The flavor of the tangerine induces a strong appetite and is a special delicacy.
* The tangerine abounds in vitamin C, which helps prevent colds and is good to recuperate from fatigue. Another agent in it, vitamin P (citrin) is effective in preventing the hypertension of blood.
* Since the tangerine accelerates the acidification of kimchi, make a small amount of it at a time. This dish goes well with Korean sweets and rice cake, *tteok*.

DIRECTIONS

1 Peel off the skin as well as the inner endodermis of the tangerines and separate their cloves from one another. (Photo 1)

2 Cut the Chinese cabbage into square pieces (3 cm×2.5 cm). Slice the radish into small pieces (3 cm×2.5 cm×0.2 cm). Pickle them lightly in the salt solution and drain. (Photo 2)

3 Cut the watercress into 3 cm lengths. Chop the fresh red peppers into 3 cm long julienne pieces. (Mince garlic and ginger if not ready yet.) (Photo 3)

4 Mix up all the ingredients and spices together, except the watercress, in the bowl. Put the mix into a crock. (Photo 4)

5 Make kimchi juice in the bowl where seasonings were mixed by adding sugar, fine salt and red pepper powder, then pour into the crock. Float some watercress on the kimchi juice when serving.

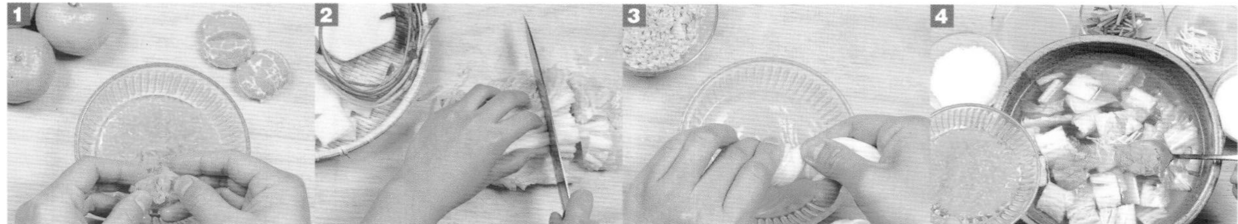

Lanceolate Kimchi
Deodeok Kimchi

A specialty of both North and South Gyeongsang province, the *deodeok* root is stuffed with seasonings in its surface slits for this dish. Loved for its crunchiness and bitter and fragrant tastes, along with its mildly salty juice, lanceolate kimchi is usually made during the spring.

Ingredients

600 g (30 ea) lanceolate (*deodeok*)
90 g (4 Tss) coarse salt
200 g Chinese chive (*buchu*)
40 g (1/2 cup) red pepper powder
160 g (2 stalks) Welsh onion
90 g (1/3 cup) pickled baby shrimp
25 g (1/2 head) minced garlic
15 g minced ginger
15 g (1 Ts) sugar, 5 g (1ts) fine salt

Tips

* Pickle the *deodeok* enough to prevent it from breaking when slit-cut.
* Be sure not to spoil the surface of the *deodeok* with the stuffing, so as to craft a better look.
* Use chopsticks when inserting the stuffing to keep the surface of the *deodeok* from being ripped apart.
* The lanceolate root builds physical strength and effectively reduces fatigue. It also lowers hypertension and strengthens the physiological function of the lungs, whereby bronchitis may be prevented.

Directions

1 Peel off the outer crust of the *deodeok*, which should be thick and straight. Wash and cut them into 5 cm lengths. Slit cut each one lengthwise, leaving 1 cm on both ends, and then pickle. (Photo 1)

2 Cut the Chinese chive into 2 cm lengths. Take the pickled baby shrimp out of the pickle juice and mince them. Soak the red pepper powder in a cup of lukewarm water that is 1/3 full. (Photo 2)

3 Place all the lanceolate roots in a cloth and bind it. Place a rock over the bundle. Mix in the soaked red pepper powder, pickled baby shrimp and Welsh onion, garlic and ginger. Then add the Chinese chive to it to make the stuffing. (Photo 3)

4 Insert the stuffing into the slits of each *deodeok*, then stack them in a crock tightly. Pour water into the mixing vessel to gather the residual seasoning of the stuffing. Adjust its taste with sugar and fine salt. Pour the juice into the crock. (Photo 4)

1. Turnip Radish Watery Kimchi
2. Eggplant Kimchi
3. Green Bean Kimchi
4. Carrot Kimchi
5. Rucola Kimchi
6. Cube Broccoli Radish Kimchi
7. Broccoli Watery Kimchi
8. Green Vitamin Kimchi
9. Green Vitamin Watery Kimchi
10. Cube Celery and Radish Kimchi
11. Celery Watery Kimchi
12. Asparagus Kimchi
13. Cube Yacon Kimchi
14. Cabbage Kimchi
15. Cabbage Watery Kimchi
16. Endive Kimchi
17. Chicon Watery Kimchi
18. Cauliflower Kimchi
19. Cauliflower Watery Kimchi
20. Pimento Kimchi

Turnip Radish Watery Kimchi

The rainbow colored turnip radish is cut into triangular pieces like folding fans and fermented without red pepper.

INGREDIENTS

200 g turnip radish
10 g (1 Ts) fine salt for pickling turnip radish
5 g threaded green onion
3 g thin-sliced garlic, 1 g thin-sliced ginger
kimchi juice [0.6 *l* (3 cups) water+7.5 g (1/2 Ts) fine salt+15 g (1 Ts) sugar]

TIPS

* Choose a medium sized turnip radish.
* The reason why red pepper isn't added is that turnip radish's own gorgeous colors are best kept intact.
* Over-fermented Turnip radish kimchi loses its lustrous color, making it look like white radish.
* The red color of the turnip radish induces appetites, while being aesthetically appealing at the same time.

DIRECTIONS

1 Wash the turnip radish and peel off its outer crust. Cut it into 0.3 cm thick triangular pieces. Pickle and drain. Preserve the remaining brine for later use.

2 Cut the threaded green onion into 3 cm long pieces.

3 Mix in all the materials together, adjusting the taste with fine salt. Put the mix into a kimchi container, pressing hard to remove any air pockets.

4 Add water to the brine to make kimchi juice, adjusting taste with fine salt and sugar. Pour the kimchi juice into a kimchi container. This kimchi dish requires 3-4 days before it reaches its optimal fermentation.

Eggplant Kimchi

Small eggplants are pickled and then mixed with fresh green and red pimentos for this dish.

INGREDIENTS

500 g small eggplant
22.5 g (1½ Ts) fine salt for pickling eggplant
20 g green pimento, 20 g red pimento
9 g (1½ Tss) red pepper powder
3 g minced garlic, 1 g thin-sliced ginger
10 g (1 Ts) fine salt, 15 g (1 Ts) sugar

TIPS

* It is better to have this kimchi fermented at room temperature. Avoid a lower temperature because the eggplant may be decolored otherwise.
* To negate the astringent and acrid tastes of the eggplant, soak it in water thoroughly, boil it at over 100℃, or steam it before making it into kimchi.
* The scopoletin and scoparone elements in eggplant mitigate the tension of the nerves, especially convulsions.
* This dish is good for preventing bronchitis and tonsillitis.
* Eggplant is good for children with weak teeth and for older people.
* Spaghetti goes very well with the eggplant kimchi.

DIRECTIONS

1 Wash the eggplant and slice it into 0.5 cm thick round pieces. Pickle them lightly and drain. Save the residual brine for later use.

2 Chop the red pimento into 2 cm × 2 cm pieces. Chop the green pimento into 3 cm long julienne pieces.

3 Add the pimentos, minced garlic and thin-sliced ginger to the pickled eggplant, then mix them all in a bowl, adjusting the taste with red pepper powder, fine salt and sugar. Put the mix into a jar, pressing down hard to remove any air pockets.

4 Rinse the mixing bowl with the residual brine and pour all the juice into the jar. It shouldn't take more than a couple of days to ferment completely.

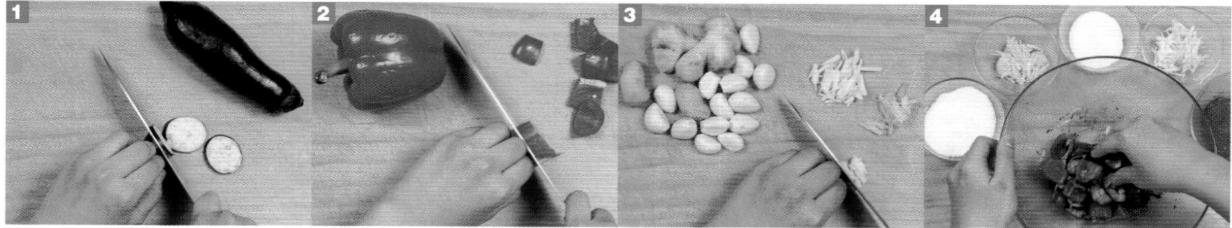

Green Bean Kimchi

Made of lightly pickled green beans and sliced radishes the size of the green beans, this dish is healthy and easy to put together.

INGREDIENTS

200 g green bean, 100 g radish
15 g (1½Tss) fine salt for green bean and radish
80 g (1 Ts) red pepper powder
3 g minced garlic, 1 g minced ginger
5 g (1 ts) fine salt, 15 g (1 Ts) sugar

TIPS

* It takes longer to pickle the green beans than other vegetables.
* It also takes longer, at least 2-3 days, for the green beans to absorb the seasonings and spices. So, wait a little longer before consuming this dish.
* Green beans abound in protein, which helps detoxification and preventing cancer.
* The color of the green beans goes well with red pepper powder.
* Green beans are chewy and have a taste all their own.

DIRECTIONS

1 Wash and remove the two hard ends of each green bean. Cut them into halves.

2 Chop the radish into the same size as the green beans, then pickle the radish pieces with the green beans and drain. Save the brine for later use.

3 Add red pepper powder, garlic and ginger to the pickled green beans and radish. Mix them all together, adjusting the taste with fine salt and sugar. Put the mix into an airtight jar.

4 Pour the residual brine into the seasoning mix bowl and then pour that into the jar. It should take 2-3 days for the kimchi to completely ferment.

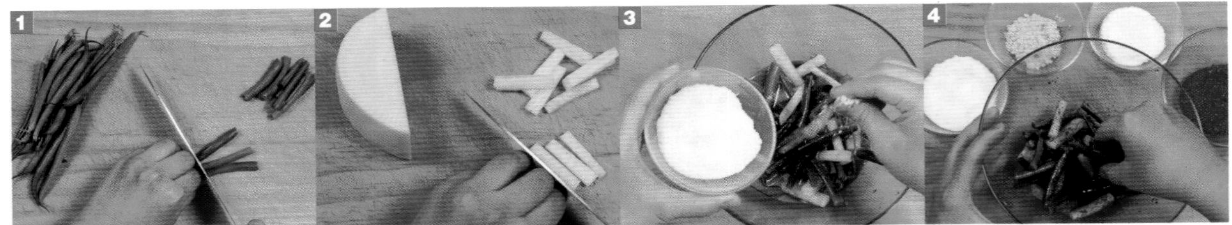

Carrot Kimchi

A mix of carrots, Chinese cabbage and several seasonings, this carrot kimchi dish is enjoyed for its crunchiness.

Ingredients

500 g (1 ea) carrot
300 g Chinese cabbage
22.5 g (1½ Tss) fine salt for pickling carrots and Chinese cabbage
30 g green pimento
3 g (1/2 Ts) red pepper powder
5 g minced garlic, 3 g minced ginger
5 g (1 ts) fine salt, 15 g (1 Ts) sugar

Tips

* There is no need to add sugar since the carrot contains some sweet element on their own. Carrot become soft easily, so only make a small quantity of carrot kimchi at a time.
* If not pickled, the carrot gives off a very strong scent.
* Carrots are a good source of vitamin A, as they turn βcarotin into vitamin A in the body.
* Carrots have been shown to slow aging, prevent cancer, strengthen vision and improve night vision.
* One can still taste the crunchiness of the carrot with this kimchi.

Directions

1 Wash the carrot and slit-cut it into quarters, lengthwise, then chop them into 0.5 cm thick slices. Chop the Chinese cabbage into 2.5 cm lengths. pickle the carrots and cabbage together, and drain. Save the remaining brine for later use.

2 Cut the green pimento into 3 cm long pieces.

3 Add the green pimento, red pepper powder, garlic and ginger to the pickled carrots and cabbage. Mix them all together, adjusting the taste with fine salt and sugar. Put the entire mix into a jar, pressing down hard to eliminate any air pockets.

4 Rinse the seasoning mix vessel with the brine saved, then pour the seasoning juice into the jar. This kimchi takes 3-4 days to ferment properly.

Rucola Kimchi

This rucola dish is pickled and then mixed with red pimento before being served.

INGREDIENTS

500 g rucola
22.5 g (1½ Tss) fine salt for pickling rucola
30 g red pimento
6 g (1 Ts) red pepper powder
3 g sliced garlic, 2 g sliced ginger
2.5 g (1/2 ts) fine salt, 15 g (1 Ts) sugar

TIPS

* Rucola has a bitter taste and scent.
* Choose rucola with vivid green leaves.
* Wash the rucola with water in a container rather than with running water.
* This rucola kimchi is enjoyed by those who like bitter tasting dishes.

DIRECTIONS

1 Pickle the pimentos lightly and drain. Save the brine for later use.

2 Chop the red pimento into 3 cm lengths, and then thinly slice them into strips.

3 Add the red pimento, red pepper powder, sliced garlic and ginger to the pickled rucola in a vessel. Mix them all together while adjusting the taste with fine salt and sugar.

4 Put the entire mix into a jar. Make kimchi juice with the brine saved and the residual seasoning mix from the bowl. Pour the juice into the kimchi jar. Fermentation usually takes about 3 days.

Cube Broccoli Radish Kimchi

After the broccoli stems are separated from each other and the radishes are cut into small cubes, they are mixed with red pimento and several seasonings.

INGREDIENTS

500 g broccoli, 200 g radish
15 g (1 Ts) fine saltfor pickling broccoli, radish and pimento
30 g red pimento
6 g (1 Ts) red pepper powder
3 g minced garlic, 1 g minced ginger
2.5 g (1/2 ts) fine salt, 10 g (2 tss) sugar

TIPS

* This cube broccoli radish dish should be consumed soon after being made since it cannot be stored for very long.
* This dish tastes best right after it is made.
* Broccoli kimchi abounds in vitamins A and C.
* The crunchiness of cube broccoli radish go well with meat dishes.

DIRECTIONS

1 Wash the broccoli and separate its stems from each other. Cut the radish into cubes (2.5 cm × 2.5 cm × 2.5 cm). Cut the pimento into 2 cm long pieces.

2 Pickle the broccoli, radish cubes and red pimento together, and then drain. Save the brine for later use.

3 Add the red pepper powder, garlic and ginger to the pickled broccoli. Put that, the radish cubes and the red pimento in a bowl. Mix thoroughly while adjusting the taste with fine salt and sugar. Put the entire mix into a jar tightly, eliminating any air pockets.

4 Pour the saved brine into the seasoning mix bowl. Rinse it in order to get as much kimchi juice as possible, and then pour it into the kimchi jar.

Broccoli Watery Kimchi

The broccoli stems are torn apart, and the separated stems further thin-sliced before red pimento is added to the broccoli, radish and kimchi juice.

INGREDIENTS

500 g broccoli, 200 g radish
45 g (3 Ts) fine salt for pickling broccoli and radish
50 g red pimento, 3 g minced garlic
2 g minced ginger
3.3 g (1 ts) pine nuts
9 g (1½ Tss) fine red pepper powder
kimchi juice [2 *l* (10 cups) water + 15 g (1 Ts) fine salt + 15 g (1Ts) sugar]

TIPS

* Since the broccoli cannot be stored very long, it is better to consume it as soon as it is harvested.
* Broccoli kimchi goes bad easily, so prepare a small amount of it at a time and consume it immediately.
* Broccoli abounds in vitamins A and C, with two times as much vitamin C as a lemon, and seven times as much as a potato. That's why it's regarded as the most excellent vitamin C source among all the vegetables.
* One can enjoy the crunchiness of broccoli watery kimchi with hamburgers.

DIRECTIONS

1 Wash the broccoli and separate its stems from each other, cutting them further into flat slices. Cut the radish into small pieces (1.5 cm × 1.5 cm × 1.5 cm), pickle them lightly and dry. Save the brine for later use.

2 Chop the red pimento into 3 cm × 3 cm pieces.

3 Add the garlic, ginger, and chopped pimentos to the pickled broccoli and radish pieces, then mix them together, adjusting the taste with fine salt and sugar. Put the entire mix into a kimchi container, pressing down tightly to eliminate any air pockets.

4 Add water to the saved brine in the mixing vessel. Put red pepper powder into a linen bag and stir it in the brine to make red kimchi juice, adjusting the taste with fine salt and sugar. Pour the kimchi juice into the kimchi container. Just one day is required for this kimchi to ferment properly. When served, try floating pine nuts on the surface of the juice.

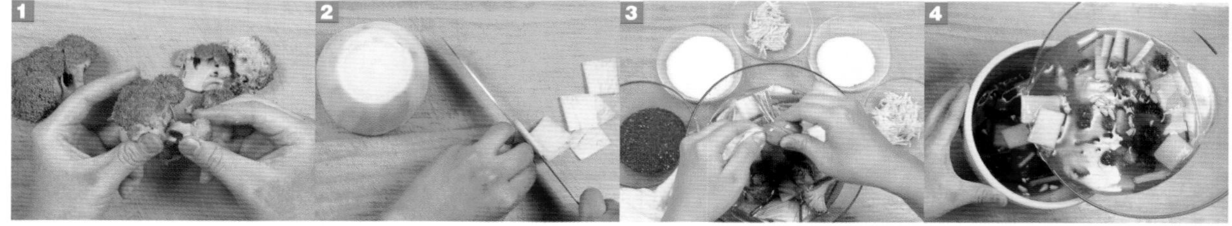

Green Vitamin Kimchi

The green vitamin in this dish is lightly pickled and mixed with the sliced red pimento and seasonings.

INGREDIENTS

400 g green vitamin
15 g (1 Ts) fine salt for pickling green vitamin
30 g red pimento
9 g (1½ Tss) red pepper powder
3 g minced garlic, 2 g minced ginger
15 g (1 Ts) sugar, 2.5 g (½ ts) fine salt

TIPS

* Choose medium sized green vitamins. Small ones that are young soon become deformed.
* Tear apart the leaves on the green vitamins by hand rather than with a knife, then rinse them in water.
* The green vitamin abounds in carotin, which eventually turns into vitamin A in the body. It contains about two times as much carotin as spinach.
* The fresh green of this dish goes well with oily food.

DIRECTIONS

1 Wash and pickle the green vitamins with fine salt, drain and dry. Save the brine for later use.

2 Chop the red pimento into 3 cm long strips.

3 Add the garlic, ginger and red pepper powder to the green vitamin in the seasoning mix bowl and then mix them thoroughly, adjusting the taste with salt and sugar. Put the entire mix into a kimchi container, pressing hard to eliminate any air pockets.

4 Pour the saved brine into the seasoning mixing bowl and rinse the residual seasonings to make the necessary kimchi juice. Pour the juice into the kimchi container, and wait for three days for the kimchi to properly ferment.

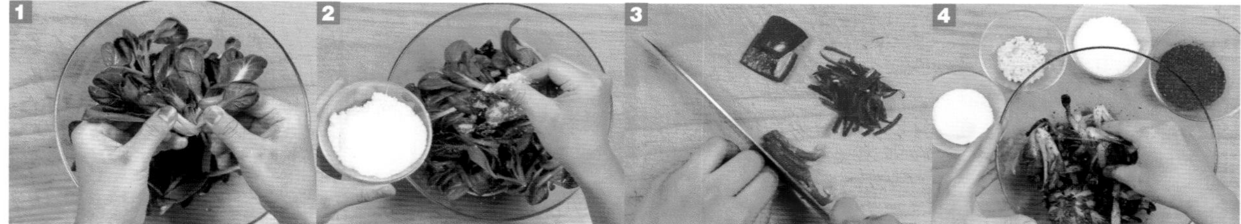

Green Vitamin Watery Kimchi

This is a watery kimchi dish that is made of green vitamins, with red pimento and seasonings added, too.

INGREDIENTS

300 g green vitamin
15 g (1 Ts) fine salt for pickling green vitamin
30 g red pimento, 3 g thin-sliced garlic
1 g thin-sliced ginger
kimchi juice [0.6 ℓ (3 cups) water + 6 g (1 Ts) fine red pepper power + 6 g (1/2 Ts) fine salt + 15 g (1 Ts) sugar]

TIPS

* Choose green vitamins with wide, elastic, lustrous green leaves.
* Do not use young green vitamins, as they become deformed easily.
* Do not use a knife when trimming green vitamins. Rather, use your hands to tear off the leaves from the stem.
* The fresh green of this dish goes well with oily food.

DIRECTIONS

1 Wash the green vitamins and cut it into bite size pieces, sousing lightly. Do not discard its brine; it will be used for kimchi juice later.
2 Chop the red pimento into 3 cm long strips.
3 Add the red pimento, garlic and ginger to the soused green vitamin in the bowl, mixing them up. Put the entire mix into the kimchi container, pressing hard to eliminate any air pockets.
4 Pour water into the mixing bowl. Put the fine red pepper powder into a linen bag and shake it well in the water to make the kimchi juice, adjusting the taste with fine salt and sugar. Pour the kimchi juice into the kimchi container. It takes about 3 days before this kimchi becomes properly fermented.

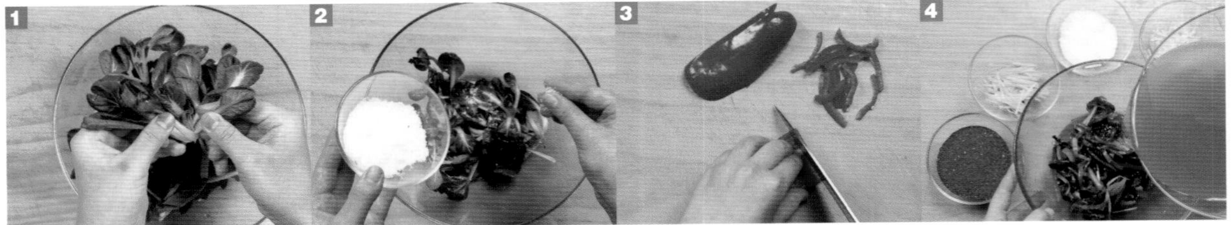

Cube Celery and Radish Kimchi

Cut the celery diagonally and cube the radish before mixing them with the seasonings.

INGREDIENTS

300 g celery, 200 g radish
22.5 g (1½ Tss) fine salt for pickling celery and radish
8 g (1 Ts) red pepper powder
5 g minced garlic, 3 g minced ginger
2.5 g (½ ts) fine salt, 15 g (1 Ts) sugar

TIPS

* Because celery is sweet and has a particular scent, it is used in various ways in a different dishes.
* The optimal length of the celery to be used is 20-25 cm from the root to the first knot. Use 14-15 heads of celery for this kimchi.
* Celery with a rounder and fatter stem and green color leaves is best.
* Celery helps mitigate body heat and stimulates the diuretic effect. Its nutrients are found in the leaves rather than in the stem, so make sure you use the leaves.
* Celery stimulates an appetite and digestion. Since it contains a lot of vegetable fiber, it is effective in preventing constipation.
* Celery and radish kimchi is crunchy and has its own particular flavor, which helps stimulate the appetite in those who are having trouble eating.

DIRECTIONS

1 Wash the celery and peel off its outer skin. Chop it diagonally into 0.5 cm thick slices.

2 Trim the radish and chop it into cubes (1.5 cm × 1.5 cm × 1.5 cm). Pickle the celery and radish cubes together, drain and dry. Save the brine for later use.

3 Add red pepper powder, garlic and ginger to the celery and the radish cubes in the mixing bowl. Mix them up, adjusting the taste with fine salt and sugar. Put the mix into a kimchi container and press hard to remove any air pockets.

4 Rinse the seasoning mix bowl with the brine saved to make the kimchi juice. Pour it into the kimchi container and leave the kimchi for 3-4 days to reach optimal fermentation.

Celery Watery Kimchi

The celery in this crunchy dish is sliced diagonally and mixed with the Chinese cabbage, red pimento and spices.

INGREDIENTS

500 g celery, 300 g Chinese cabbage
22.5 g (1½ Tss) fine salt for pickling celery and Chinese cabbage
20 g red pimento
5 g minced garlic, 3 g minced ginger
kimchi juice [2 *l* (10 cups) water + 15 g 1(Ts) fine salt + 6 g (1Ts) fine red pepper powder + 15 g (1 Ts) sugar]

TIPS

* Celery is sweet and has a particular fragrance, so it is used variously while cooking.
* Peel off the outer skin of the celery to make a tastier kimchi.
* Celery stimulates the appetite and digestion. Since it contains a lot of vegetable fiber, it helps prevent constipation.
* Celery is an alkaline vegetable and contains a lot of iron, so is good for hematosis.
* People enjoy celery watery kimchi for its particularly strong flavor.
* Celery watery kimchi goes well with oily food because it helps neutralize the fat in such food.

DIRECTIONS

1 Wash the celery and peel off its outer skin. Cut it diagonally into 0.5 cm thick slices. Chop the Chinese cabbage into 2.5 cm × 2.5 cm pieces. Pickle the celery and the cabbage together, drain and dry. Save the residual brine in order to make kimchi juice later.

2 Chop the red pimento into 3 cm long slices.

3 Add the red pimento slices, minced garlic and ginger to the soused celery and cabbage pieces in the mixing bowl. Mix them all together and then pickle. Put the entire mix into a container, pressing hard to remove any remaining air pockets.

4 Pour the brine saved and kimchi juice into the mixing bowl. Put the fine red pepper powder into a linen bag and stir it well in the kimchi juice to have the soaked fine red pepper slowly come out into the kimchi juice. Adjust the taste with fine salt and sugar. Pour the kimchi juice into a kimchi container. It takes about 3 days for this kimchi to properly ferment.

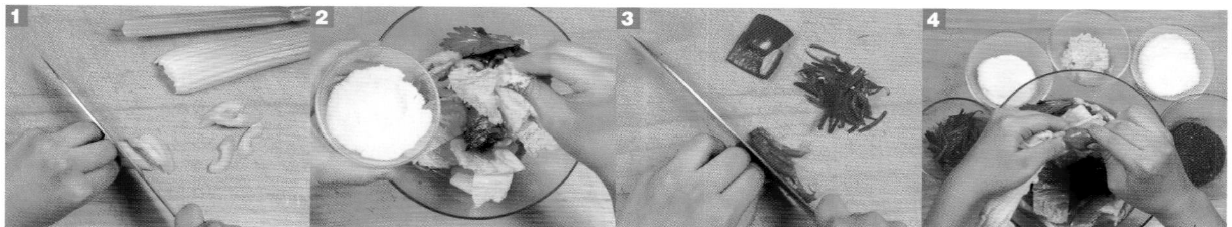

Asparagus Kimchi

The surface of asparagus is slit cut with a knife. After being pickled and drained, it is stuffed with seasonings made from radish, carrot, green pimento and other spicy ingredients.

INGREDIENTS

500 g asparagus
15 g (1 Ts) fine salt for pickling asparagus
30 g carrot, 30 g green pimento
50 g radish
6 g (1 Ts) red pepper powder
3 g thin-sliced garlic, 2 g thin-sliced ginger
2.5 g (1/2 ts) fine salt, 15 g (1 Ts) sugar

TIPS

* The bitter taste of asparagus comes from the asparagenic acid contained in it. This helps the body's metabolism and the synthesis of protein, whereby fatigue can be mitigated and the tonic effect can be heightened.
* The rutin contents in asparagus strengthen blood vessels, helping to relieve hypertension. As such, it is effective in lowering high blood pressure.
* Asparagus is soft and palatable, so goes well with any kind of food.
* Asparagus can be fried in a pan that has been coated in olive oil.

DIRECTIONS

1 Cut off the hard part of the asparagus. Trim, pickle, drain and dry. Save the brine for later use.

2 Slit cut the asparagus, leaving about 2 cm on both ends untouched.

3 Cut the carrot, green pimento and radish into 1 cm long strips. Mix them with the red pepper power and garlic and ginger slices in the seasoning mixing bowl, adjusting the taste with fine salt and sugar.

4 Insert the seasoning mix into the slit of the asparagus. Stack the asparagus in a kimchi container, pressing hard to remove any air pockets.

5 Rinse the seasoning mixing bowl with the brine saved to make the kimchi juice. Pour the juice into the kimchi container and wait 4-5 days for this kimchi to become properly fermented.

Cube Yacon Kimchi

For this dish, the yacon is chopped and made into kimchi with green pimento and other seasonings.

Ingredients

500 g yacon, 30 g green pimento
15 g (1 Ts) fine salt for pickling yacon and green pimento
6 g (1 Ts) red pepper powder
5 g thin-sliced garlic
3 g thin-sliced ginger
2.5 g (1/2 ts) fine salt

Tips

* Yacon is a perennial plant belonging to the chrysanthemum family. It looks like the sweet potato, but its top portion looks like the artichoke.
* Because the yacon contains sweet elements in it, sugar is not used in yacon *kkakdugi*.
* Since the color of its meat changes easily, immerse the yacon in water after its outer crust is peeled off.
* The yacon becomes soft easily; make a small amount of this kimchi at a time for quick consumption, enjoying its unique taste.
* The yacon abounds in inulin, which is effective against diabetes and poly-saccharose. Its alkaline dietary fiber is good for digestion tracts.
* Many children quickly develop a liking for *kkakdugi* kimchi.

Directions

1 Chop the yacon into small pieces (2.5 cm × 2.5 cm × 0.5 cm). Chop the green pimento so it's the same size as the yacon, then pickle and drain. Save the brine for later use.

2 Add the thin-sliced garlic and ginger and red pepper powder to the pickled yacon and green pimento. Mix them up in the mixing bowl and adjust the taste with fine salt. Put the entire mix into a kimchi container, pressing hard to remove any air pockets.

3 Rinse the seasoning mixing bowl with the brine saved to make the kimchi juice, then pour the juice into the kimchi container. One day is enough for this dish to ferment.

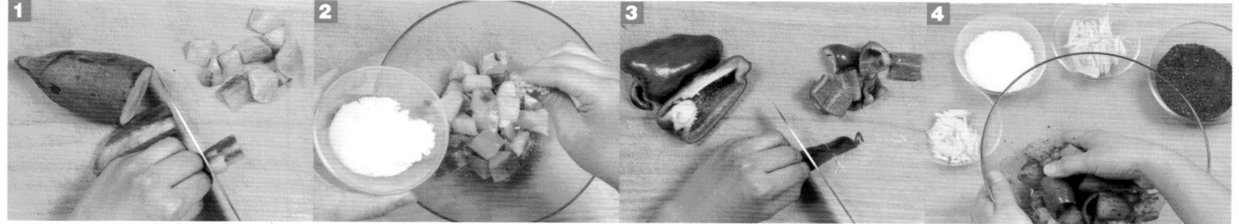

Cabbage Kimchi

The chopped cabbage pieces are pickled and mixed with carrot and seasonings in this dish.

INGREDIENTS

500 g cabbage
20 g carrot, 30 g threaded green onion
22.5 g (1½ Tss) fine salt for pickling babbage
6 g (1 Ts) red pepper power
3 g thin-sliced garlic
2 g thin-sliced ginger
2.5 g (1/2 ts) fine salt, 15 g (1 Ts) sugar

TIPS

* It takes longer to pickle cabbage, because its leaves are hard.
* Cabbage is a good alkaline food for growing children because it abounds in essential amino acids, including basic lysine.
* Cabbage is good for mitigating stomach ulcers and diabetes, and also for lowering high blood pressure.
* With this kimchi you can have the sweet taste of cabbage and the hot taste of red pepper simultaneously. This dish also goes well with many other things.

DIRECTIONS

1 Cut the cabbage into 3 cm × 3 cm pieces, wash, pickle and drain.

2 Chop the carrot into small pieces (3 cm × 3 cm × 0.5 cm), pickle and dry. Save the residual brine for later use. Cut the threaded green onion into 3 cm lengths.

3 Add the red pepper powder, garlic and ginger to the pickled cabbage and carrot pieces in the mixing bowl and mix them up, adjusting the taste with fine salt and sugar. Put the entire mix into a kimchi container, pressing hard to eliminate any air pockets.

4 Rinse the mixing bowl with the brine saved, then pour the juice into the kimchi container. Wait 3-4 days for the kimchi to properly ferment.

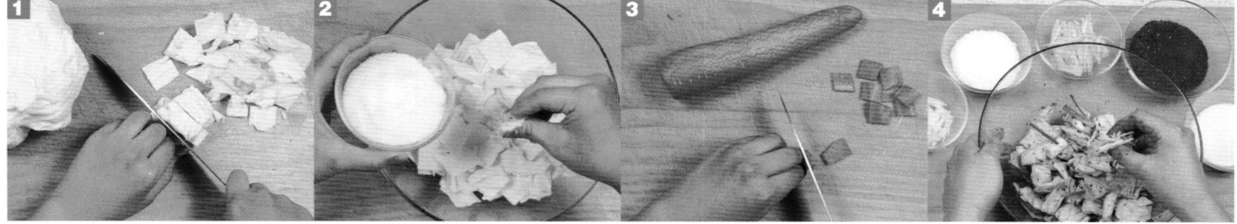

Cabbage Watery Kimchi

This is a watery kimchi dish made of cabbage, carrot and pimento—all mixed together to bring about a unique taste.

INGREDIENTS

300 g cabbage
30 g green pimento, 30 g carrot
12 g (1 Ts) fine salt for cabbage and carrot
3 g thin-sliced garlic
1 g thin-sliced ginger
kimchi juice [1 ℓ (5 cups) water + 15 g (1 Ts) fine salt + 6 g (1 Ts) fine red pepper power + 15 g (1 Ts) sugar]

TIPS

* Since cabbage is an alkaline food, it helps the absorption of calcium in the body.
* Noodles go well with this kimchi juice. It also goes well with oily food, meat, and bread.

DIRECTIONS

1 Cut the cabbage and the green pimento into 2.5 cm×2.5 cm pieces. Slice the carrot into small pieces (2.5 cm×2.5 cm×0.5 cm). When the cabbage pieces are pickled, add the carrot pieces to it for further but light pickling. Drain and save the brine for later use.

2 Put the pickled cabbage and carrot pieces, green pimento, and thin-sliced garlic and ginger into the mixing bowl, mix them up, and adjust the taste with fine salt and sugar. Put the entire mix into a kimchi container, pressing hard to eliminate any air pockets.

3 Put fine red pepper powder into a linen bag, stirring it in water to make the kimchi juice in the mixing vessel. Add the brine saved to the kimchi juice, adjusting the taste with fine salt and sugar, then pour the kimchi juice into the kimchi container. Wait 3-4 days for the kimchi to become properly fermented.

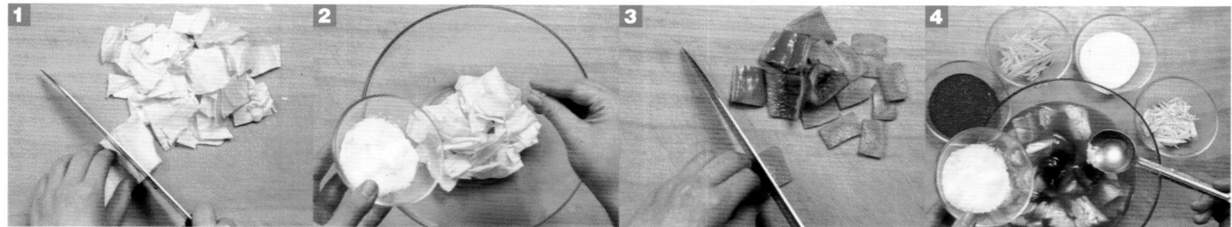

Endive Kimchi

This dish is made of endive, green pimento and assorted seasonings.

INGREDIENTS

500 g endive
15 g (1 Ts) fine salt for pickling endive
1 l (5 cups) water, 30 g green pimento
6 g (1 Ts) fine red pepper powder
5 g minced garlic, 3 g minced ginger
2.5 g (1/2 ts) fine salt, 10 g (2 tss) sugar

TIPS

* Some people might know endive by its other name, chichory.
* Endive abounds in carotin and iron.
* Do not keep endive immersed in water long, because it will become deformed and tasteless.
* This kimchi tastes sweet when well-fermented but eventually turns a little bitter.
* This dish goes well with oily duck meat and meat.

DIRECTIONS

1 Chop the endive into 2.5 cm lengths, pickle and drain. Save the brine for later use.

2 Chop the green pimento into 3 cm long strips.

3 Add the green pimento, garlic, ginger and red pepper powder to the pickled endive, then mix them together in the mixing bowl, adjusting the taste with fine salt and sugar. Put the entire mix into a kimchi container, pressing hard to eliminate any air pockets.

4 Rinse the mixing bowl with the brine saved, and pour the juice into the kimchi container. Wait 3-4 days for the kimchi to become properly fermented.

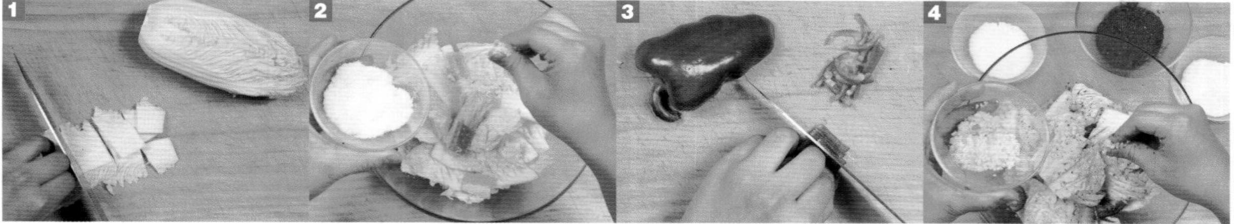

Chicon Watery Kimchi

The chicon in this dish is lightly pickled and then mixed with the green pimento and other seasonings.

INGREDIENTS

200 g chicon
7.5 g (1/2 Ts) fine salt for pickling chicon
30 g green pimento, 3 g thin-sliced garlic
1 g thin-sliced ginger
kimchi juice [0.6 ℓ (3 cups) water + 7.5 g (1/2 Ts) fine salt + 3 g (1/2 Ts) fine red pepper powder + 15 g (1 Ts) sugar]

TIPS

* Chicon takes a little longer than average to pickle.
* The bitter taste of chicon comes from the intybin in it, which stimulates digestion and strengthens blood vessels. Chicon goes well with meat dishes.

DIRECTIONS

1 Chop the chicon into 2.5 cm lengths, pickle lightly and drain. Discard the residual brine, since it tastes too bitter.
2 Thinly slice the green pimento into 3 cm long strips.
3 Add the green pimento strips, thin-sliced garlic and ginger to the chicon pieces, mix them all in the mixing bowl, and adjust the taste with fine salt and sugar. Put the entire mix into a kimchi container.
4 Rinse the mixing bowl with water to make the seasoning juice. Put fine red pepper powder into a linen bag and stir it in water, then pour it into the seasoning juice, adjusting the taste with fine salt and sugar. Pour the juice into the kimchi container. Wait 3-4 days for it to become properly fermented.

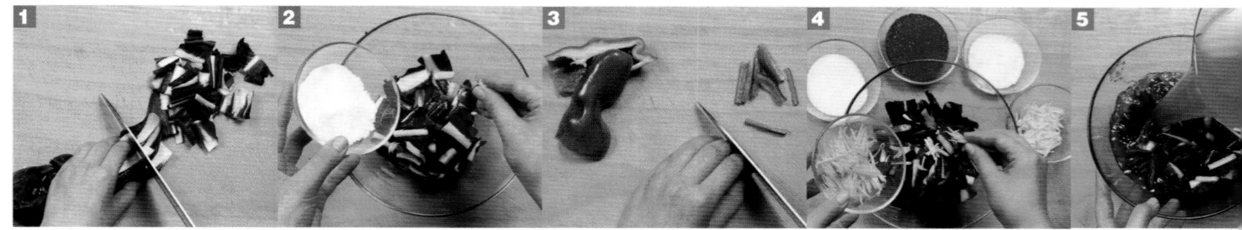

Cauliflower Kimchi

Cauliflower kimchi is made after its stems are torn apart and is then mixed with carrot and celery pieces .

INGREDIENTS

500 g cauliflower, 20 g carrot, 30 g celery
9 g (1½ Tss) fine salt for pickling cauliflower and carrot
6 g (1 Ts) red pepper powder
5 g minced garlic, 3 g minced ginger
2.5 g (1/2 ts) fine salt, 15 g (1 Ts) sugar

TIPS

* Cauliflower is a variety of the cabbage, which tastes best when harvested between the autumn and the spring.
* When the cauliflower is immersed in boiling water with vinegar or lemon it becomes whiter and cleaner.
* Cauliflower contains a lot of vitamin C, which is not lost in boiling water.
* This dish brings out the softness of cauliflower and the pungency of red pepper.

DIRECTIONS

1 The stems of the cauliflower are torn apart and then sliced flat. Chop the carrot into small pieces (2 cm × 2 cm × 0.5 cm). Pickle both vegetables and drain. Save the brine for later use. Thinly slice the celery.

2 Add the celery, garlic, ginger and red pepper powder to the pickled cauliflower and carrot pieces and mix them up in the mixing bowl, adjusting the taste with fine salt and sugar. Put the entire mix into a kimchi container, pressing hard to eliminate any air pockets.

3 Rinse the mixing bowl with the brine saved to make kimchi juice. Pour the kimchi juice into the kimchi container. This dish requires a couple of days to ferment properly.

Cauliflower Watery Kimchi

Cauliflower watery kimchi is made after its stems are torn apart, pickled and mixed with carrot, as well as green and red pimentos.

INGREDIENTS

500 g cauliflower, 20 g carrot
22.5 g (1½ Tss) fine salt for pickling cauliflower and carrot
8 g (1 Ts) fine red pepper powder
10 g red pimento, 10 g green pimento
3 g thin-sliced garlic
1 g thin-sliced ginger
3.3 g (1 ts) pine nuts
kimchi juice [1 *l* (5 cups) water + 15 g (1 Ts) fine salt + 6 g (1 Ts) fine red pepper powder + 15 g (1 Ts) sugar]

TIPS

* Cauliflower watery kimchi becomes decolored in 10 days even if it is stored at room temperature or in a refrigerator.
* Cauliflower is said to be effective against colon, rectal, stomach, prostate and urinary bladder cancer.
* You can do without pine nuts if they are not available.
* Since this watery kimchi is not very hot, try serving it as a refreshing side dish to those who are not used to having spicy food.
* Noodles go well with cauliflower kimchi juice. Soaked noodles in kimchi juice offer a fresh and very palatable taste.

DIRECTIONS

1 Tear off each stem of the cauliflower and then cut it flat. Chop the carrot into small pieces (2 cm × 2 cm × 0.3 cm). Pickle both the cauliflower and carrot pieces lightly and drain. Save the brine for later use.

2 Chop the green and red pimentos into 3 cm long thin strips.

3 Add the green and red pimentos, garlic, and ginger to the cauliflower and carrot pieces, mixing them up in the mixing bowl. Put the entire mix into a kimchi container, pressing hard to eliminate any air pockets.

4 Rinse the mixing bowl with the brine saved. Add water to it, then stir the linen bag with fine red pepper in it, adjusting the taste with fine salt and sugar to make the kimchi juice. Pour the kimchi juice into the kimchi container. Wait a couple of days for it to become properly fermented.

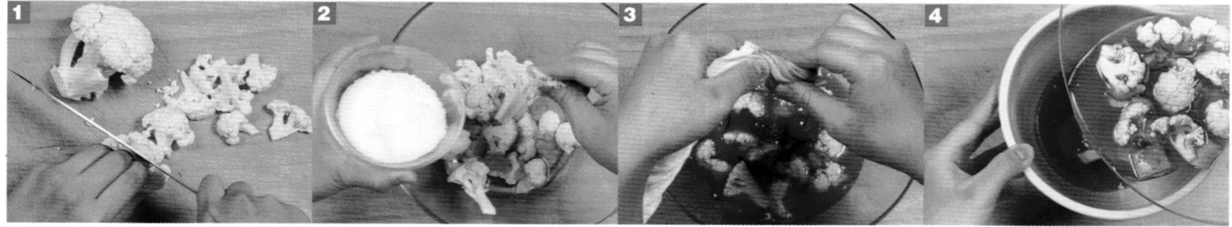

Pimento Kimchi

The green pimento is cut into square pieces and mixed together with the carrot pieces and assorted spices for this dish.

INGREDIENTS

500 g green pimento, 30 g carrot
10 g (1 Ts) fine salt for pickling green pmento and carrot
8 g (1 Ts) red pepper powder
3 g thin-sliced garlic
1 g thin-sliced ginger
2.5 g (1/2 ts) fine salt, 15 g (1 Ts) sugar

TIPS

* The pimento helps stimulate metabolism in the body, helping purify it in the process.
* Besides the crunchiness and the flavor of the pimento, this kimchi has both a sweet and spicy taste to it.
* Pimento kimchi goes well with beef and roast chicken, helping the digestion of both.

DIRECTIONS

1 Chop the green pimento and carrots into small pieces (2 cm × 2 cm × 0.3 cm). Pickle and drain. Save the brine for later use.

2 Add the red pepper powder, thin-sliced garlic and ginger to the pickled pimento and carrot pieces, then mix them up in the mixing bowl, adjusting the taste with fine salt and sugar. Put the mix into a kimchi container, pressing hard to remove any air pockets.

3 Rinse the mixing bowl with the brine saved, and then pour it into the kimchi container. It takes a couple of days for it to become properly fermented.

References

Choi, E-soon; Lee, Ki-yull (1977) *Practical Korean Recipes*. Seoul: Yonsei University Press.

Chu, Woul-young (1985) *Traditional Korean Cuisine*. Los Angeles: The Korea Times L.A.

Lee, Florence C. & Lee, Helen C. (1988) *Kimchi*. Elizabeth, New Jersey: Hollym International Corp.

Kim, Kwi-young; Lee, Chun-ja; Park, Hye-won (1999) *The Book of Kimchi*. Translated into English by Young Ok Kim. Seoul: Korean Overseas Information Service.

Yoon, Sook-ja (2000) *Korean Seasonal Food*. Seoul: Jigu Publishers. [in Korean]

Yoon, Sook-ja (2003) *Good Morning, Kimchi!: 111 Kinds of Kimchi*. Seoul: Jilsiru. [in Korean]

Translator

Young-hie Han won his Ph.D. in English linguistics from Korea University and was a long time professor at Dankook University in Seoul. He translated Prof. Sook-Ja Yoon's *Korean Desserts: Ricecakes, Cookies and Beverages* into English, and is currently working on compiling *A Korean-English Culinary Term Dictionary*.

(e-mail: damby424@paran.com)

INDEX